KU-400-106

MacGillivray
on
Insurance Law

First Supplement to the
Tenth Edition

Up to date to October, 2005

AUSTRALIA
Law Book Co.
Sydney

CANADA
Carswell
Toronto

HONG KONG
Sweet & Maxwell Asia

NEW ZEALAND
Brookers
Wellington

SINGAPORE and MALAYSIA
Sweet & Maxwell Asia
Singapore and Kuala Lumpur

MacGillivray
on
Insurance Law

relating to all risks other than marine

First Supplement to the Tenth Edition

NICHOLAS LEGH-JONES, M.A. (Oxon.)
Of Lincoln's Inn and of the Middle Temple,
One of Her Majesty's Counsel
Visiting professor at
King's College in the University of London

JOHN BIRDS, LL.M.
Professor of Commercial Law at the University of
Sheffield

London
Sweet & Maxwell
2005

Mainwork Tenth Edition 2002
By Nicholas Legh-Jones Q.C.,
John Birds and David Owen
(ISBN 0 421 704306)

First Supplement to the Tenth Edition (2005)
By Nicholas Legh-Jones Q.C. and John Birds

Published by
Sweet & Maxwell Limited of
100 Avenue Road, Swiss Cottage, London NW3 3PF
(http://www.sweetandmaxwell.co.uk)

Typeset by YHT Ltd
Printed and bound in Great Britain by
Athenaeum Press Ltd, Gateshead

*No natural forests were destroyed to make this product;
only farmed timber was used and replanted*

A CIP catalogue record for this book is available from the British
Library

ISBN 0 421 877308

All rights reserved. Crown copyright material is reproduced with the
permission of the Controller of HMSO and the Queen's Printer for
Scotland.

No part of this publication may be reproduced or transmitted in any
form or by any means, or stored in any retrieval system of any nature
without prior written permission, except for permitted fair dealing under
the Copyright, Designs and Patents Act 1988, or in accordance with the
terms of a licence issued by the Copyright Licensing Agency in respect of
photocopying and/or reprographic reproduction. Application for
permission for other use of copyright material including permission to
reproduce extracts in other published works shall be made to the
publishers. Full acknowledgment of author, publisher and source must
be given.

© Sweet & Maxwell 2005

HOW TO USE THIS SUPPLEMENT

This is the First Supplement to the Tenth Edition of *MacGillivray on Insurance Law*, and has been compiled according to the structure of the main volume.

At the beginning of each chapter of this Supplement the mini table of contents from the main volume has been included. Where a heading in this table of contents has been marked by the symbol ■, there is relevant information included in *this* Supplement to which you should refer.

Within each chapter, updating information is referenced to the relevant paragraph in the main volume.

TABLE OF CASES

TABLE OF STATUTES

TABLE OF STATUTORY INSTRUMENTS

TABLE OF EUROPEAN LEGISLATION

CHAPTER 1

DEFINITION OF INSURANCE AND INSURABLE INTEREST

1. INTRODUCTION

Delete existing text and replace as follows:

"Contract of Insurance"—definition. A satisfactory definition of "con- **1–1** tract of insurance" is elusive, but the use of the phrase to define the ambit of fiscal and regulatory legislation has made the task of attempting it inescapable. The complex system of supervision, control and regulation created by the Financial Services and Markets Act 2000 applies to specified "regulated activities". These include effecting and carrying out, as principal, a contract of insurance—Financial Services and Markets Act (Regulated Activities) Order 2001 (S.I. 2001 No. 544), Article 10. While Article 3 states that "contract of insurance" where referred to in the Order means any contract of insurance which is either a contract of long-term insurance or a contract of general insurance falling inside the classes of actual or deemed insurance business listed in Schedule I to the Order, it does not set out any criteria for determining whether a particular contract is one of insurance in the first place, and can therefore rank for inclusion in the Schedule. The common law authorities defining the essential characteristics of an insurance contract therefore remain relevant, as is recognised by the Financial Services Authority (FSA)—*The Authorisation Manual* App. 6, paragraph 6.3.2. In this Appendix the FSA has published guidance on the identification of contracts of insurance for regulatory purposes. It came into effect on 1 August 2004 when the FSA published its *Identification of Contracts of Insurance Instrument 2004* pursuant to powers contained in the Financial Services and Markets Act 2000, s.157(1). While this is intended to provide guidance as to how the FSA will determine from its own understanding of the case law whether a given business arrangement constitutes insurance within its regulatory remit, it is accepted that in a disputed case the decision will be one for the courts—App. 6 paragraph 6.4.1.

Add new paragraph as follows:

1–1A   A useful working definition is that given by Channell J. in *Prudential Insurance Company v. Inland Revenue Commissioners* [1904] 2 K.B. 658, according to which a contract of insurance is one whereby one party (the "insurer") promises in return for a money consideration (the "premium") to pay to the other party (the "assured") a sum of money or provide him with some corresponding benefit, upon the occurrence of one or more specified events. It is necessary to elaborate the elements of this definition.

Add to end of paragraph:

1–2   **"Premium."** Where the rules of an employers' mutual insurance society required a member to reimburse the society for sums paid during an initial fixed period to indemnify him for periodical payments he was liable to make to an injured employee, this was described as part of the consideration given by the member in return for the promise of an indemnity and therefore in a sense a premium—*Wooding v. Monmouthshire & South Wales Mutual Indemnity Society* [1938] 3 All E.R. 625, 629–630; [1939] 4 All E.R. 570.

Add new paragraph as follows:

1–8A   In paragraph 6.6.7 of its *Guidance for the Identification of Insurance Contracts Instrument*, made in August 2004 (see paragraph 1 above) the FSA appears to have departed from the "principal object" test as the criterion for determining whether a contract containing both insurance and non-insurance elements is to be treated as a contract of insurance, and to have substituted for it the test of whether the contract contains "an identifiable and distinct obligation that is, in substance, an insurance obligation"—paragraph 6.6.7(1). Although the reader is referred to paragraph 6.5.4 for a definition of "insurance obligation", this is not expressly defined in that paragraph, and it must have been intended to refer to paragraph 6.3.4 where there is a description of a contract of insurance, namely, one by which a provider for a monetary consideration undertakes to pay money or to provide a benefit in response to an uncertain event adverse to the interest

2

of the recipient. "Insurance obligation" can be taken as shorthand for such an undertaking. Paragraph 6.6.7(2) then provides that the presence of an insurance obligation will mean that the main contract is a contract of insurance, whether or not that obligation is substantial in comparison with the other obligations in the contract. Given the width of the definition of "insurance obligation" which removes the distinction, for example, between insurance and guarantee, the FSA will find insurance in unexpected places. Thus a construction or hiring contract containing an express indemnity clause will arguably become a contract of insurance. A contract for the provision of services containing a clause whereby the service provider agrees, in return for an additional charge, to waive its right to payment for a period following the occurrence of an uncertain event affecting the ability of the recipient to maintain its stipulated payments, would also appear to attract regulation by the FSA, unless it could be said that the benefit provided was not "distinct" from the contractual pricing provisions, but rather a part of them. A sale contract containing a retailer's warranty would also become an insurance contract were it not for a specific exception made in paragraph 6.7.9, and in paragraph 6.7.12 the FSA says that it is likely to classify a sale contract containing an unusually extensive warranty or one provided by a third party as a contract of insurance.

It is surely doubtful whether Parliament ever intended the regulation of insurance contracts to embrace such diverse agreements, and it is submitted that the principal object test should be preferred to the approach adopted by the FSA.

Add new paragraph as follows:

Shifting and distribution of the risk. Courts in the United States have   **1–9A**
emphasised the shifting of risk from assured to underwriter and the distribution of the cost of losses among a wider community as primary elements of a contract of insurance—*Group Life & Health Insurance Co v. Royal Drug Co* 440 U.S. 205 (1979); *Union Labor Life Insurance Co v. Pireno* 458 U.S. 119 (1982). Less emphasis has been placed by English courts on these social benefits of insurance, but it has been stated that the underwriting by a mutual insurance society of its members' liabilities on terms that the society was entitled to recoup all its payments by means of additional calls levied from those who had been indemnified was not insurance in the accepted meaning of the word, although the society must have been running the risk of a member's possible insolvency—*Pailin v. Northern Employers Mutual Indemnity Co* [1925] 2 K.B. 73, 94–95. Where, however, a mutual society's rules entitled it to be reimbursed by each member for payments made to him during an initial fixed period, following which the member's remaining liability was valued and a "final call" was paid by him to the society in that amount, the fact that the society then took the risk that

3

the member's ultimate liability might exceed the final call made their relationship a contract of insurance—*Wooding v. Monmouthshire & South Wales Mutual Indemnity Society* [1939] 4 All E.R. 570. So too where an Act of Parliament required employers to be fully insured against their liability towards their employees in respect of bodily injury and disease, and a corporate employer agreed with its insurers that it would pay the full cost of the handling and disposal of claims made by employees in respect of asbestosis and mesothelioma, the fact that the insurers were held nonetheless to have assumed the risk of the company's insolvency was sufficient to maintain the character of the policy as a contract of liability insurance in conformity with the Act—*Turner & Newall v. Royal Sun Alliance Insurance Co* [2003] 2 All E.R. (Comm) 939. It was stated in the first two decisions cited above that insurance involves the insurer in accepting the risk of loss which is uncertain, this reflecting the aleatory character of insurance. Life assurance may be an exception. In *Fuji Finance Inc v. Aetna Life Insurance Co* [1997] Ch. 173, the Court of Appeal approved a definition of life assurance which applied even to cases where the amount of money payable by the insurers could not exceed the amount paid by the assured. It was said that it sufficed that money or other benefit was payable on an event which was uncertain and depended on the duration of human life. (See paragraph 1–68 below). The distinction may be that the object of life insurance cover is not so much to spread the risk of loss as in indemnity insurance, but rather to provide an investment or financial security for the beneficiary of the insurance.

Add to n.40:

1–15   **Valued policies.** *Thor Navigation Inc v. Ingosstrakh Insurance* [2005] Lloyd's Rep. I.R. 490.

Add to n.51:

1–17   **Statutory requirements.** *Feasey v. Sun Life Assurance of Canada* [2003] 2 All E.R. (Comm) 587, at [97], [121] and [145].

2. THE ENGLISH STATUTES

(c) *The Life Assurance Act 1774*

Add to n.3:

Section 3 and quantum of interest. *Feasey v. Sun Life Assurance of Canada*   **1–34**
[2003] 2 All E.R. (Comm) 587, [73].

Add to n.4:
The value of the assured's interest in the life or lives insured will be assessed on a "worst case" basis and it is sufficient if, at the date the policy is taken out, the maximum loss which the assured might suffer on the death or deaths, exceeds the sum insured thereunder—*Feasey v. Sun Life Assurance of Canada* [2003] 2 All E.R. (Comm) 587, [104].

Delete the second sub-paragraph and replace with the following text:
The decision in *Hebdon* was doubted in *Feasey v. Sun Life Assurance* at first instance—[2002] 2 All E.R. (Comm) 492—on the grounds that it was inconsistent with the decision in *Dalby v. India & London Life Assurance* (1854) 15 C.B. 365. On appeal, Waller L.J. was inclined to think that this criticism was unjustified—*Feasey v. Sun Life Assurance* [2003] 2 All E.R. (Comm) 587, [77]. The rule from *Dalby* is simply that the assured must show the existence and value of a pecuniary interest at the time the policy was effected, and cannot recover more than that amount. The assured in *Hebdon* failed to recover anything under his second policy because the court assessed the true value of his interest in his employer's life at £3,000 and that had been already amply covered by the first policy at the time when the second one was effected. He was fortunate in recovering more than that sum under the first policy.

(d) *The Gaming Act 1845*

Delete the text after n.18 and replace with the following:
It is submitted that the absence of a valid insurable interest does not by   **1–37**
itself make the contract one by way of gaming and wagering. For instance, the mere expectation of future benefit from property is insufficient to create a valid insurable interest in it (see paragraphs 1–50 to 1–51 below), but if the expectation is well-founded the insurance on the property will not be one of gaming and wagering. The Marine Insurance Act 1906, s.4(2) (a) makes clear that if an assured has no insurable interest at the time of entering into a contract of marine insurance, it will not be one by way of gaming or

wagering if he possesses an expectation of acquiring an interest. Conversely, the possession of an interest sufficient to take the insurance outside the Gaming Act 1845 does not necessarily mean that the assured has a valid insurable interest in the subject-matter of the insurance. *Dicta* to the effect that if, the assured has sufficient interest in the subject-matter of an insurance to prevent it being a gaming contract, then he must have a valid insurable interest and can enforce the contract—*Sharp v. Sphere Drake Insurance plc* [1992] 2 Lloyd's Rep. 501, 510—were cited without disapproval in *O'Kane v. Jones* [2004] 1 Lloyd's Rep. 389, 418, but have been disapproved by the Court of Appeal in *Feasey v. Sun Life Assurance* [2003] 2 All E.R. (Comm) 587,[56]–[58],[149]–[150]. The plea of want of insurable interest is distinct from one that the assured is gaming and wagering—*Macaura v. Northern Assurance Co* [1925] A.C. 619, 632—even if in an extreme case such as *Newbury International v. Reliance National Insurance Co* [1994] 1 Lloyd's Rep. 83, the insurer might run either defence.

4. GENERAL DEFINITION OF INSURABLE INTEREST

Delete existing text and replace with following:

1–49   **Working definition.** All previous editions of this work have provided the following "good working definition" applicable to all risks under the Life Assurance Act ("the Act") 1774:

> "Where the assured is so situated that the happening of the event on which the insurance money is to become payable would, as a proximate cause, involve the assured in the loss or diminution of any right recognised by law or in any legal liability there is an insurable interest in the happening of that event to the extent of the possible loss or liability".

This definition was formulated at a time when it was believed that the Act applied to insurances of real property and other indemnity insurances, whereas it now applies for practical purposes only to life, accident and other contingency insurances—see paragraph 1–27 above and paragraph 1–162 below. While it is useful in emphasising the general rule that a mere expectation of benefit from the continued preservation of the subject-matter of the insurance does not of itself create a valid insurable interest in it, it obscures the reality that it is difficult to provide a definition of insurable interest applicable in all situations—*Feasey v. Sun Life Assurance of Canada* [2003] 2 All E.R. (Comm) 587 [71]. At this juncture it suffices to note the general definition of interest as applied to life and property insurances, which are considered in detail later in this Chapter.

Add new paragraphs as follows:

Life insurance. In life insurance there is no requirement that the assured should have a legal or equitable interest in the life insured—*Feasey v. Sun Life Assurance of Canada* [2003] 2 All E.R. (Comm) 587 [124]—although this expression is sometimes used as legal shorthand. His interest is rather in the duration of the life insured, being in such a legal relationship to the life that on the latter's death, he will or may suffer the loss or diminution of some right recognised by law or be placed under some legal liability. Thus, an assured who has purchased a legacy contingent upon the legatee living to a certain age, has an insurable interest in the life of the legatee—*Law v. London Indisputable Life Policy Co* (1855) 1 K. & J. 223, and a life insurer has an interest in the duration of the life insured for the purpose of a reinsurance because he will be liable to pay the sum insured when the life drops—*Dalby v. India & London Life Insurance Co.* (1854) 15 C.B. 365. It has recently been held that an assured can have an insurable interest in the lives and physical well-being of a group of persons when their death or injury may result in the assured becoming liable to indemnify their employer for compensation payable to them or their dependants—*Feasey v. Sun Life Assurance Co of Canada* [2003] 2 All E.R. (Comm) 587, considered in paragraphs 1–93A to 1–93D below.

1–49A

Property insurance. In property insurance, a legal title to or other right in the insured property is frequently a valid source of insurable interest in it and in such cases it may be accurate to describe the assured's interest as a legal or equitable interest in the subject-matter. However, this is not the exclusive source of an insurable interest, and the assured may derive an interest in insured property from being a party to a contract relating to it, whereby the destruction or loss of the property will result either in the loss of the enjoyment of a right recognised at law, or in the diminution of the value of the right or in the incurring of a legal liability. Thus (1) a contractor whose right to remuneration for work on part of a construction project depends upon the safe completion of the project, will have an insurable interest in the whole contract works—*Deepak Fertilisers & Petrochemicals Ltd v. Davy McKee (London) Ltd* [1999] 1 All E.R. (Comm) 69; (2) a person who possesses a legal right to the exclusive use and control of a yacht owned by another for his own purposes has an insurable interest in the yacht—*Sharp v. Sphere Drake Insurance plc* [1992] 2 Lloyd's Rep. 501, 512 and (3) managing agents and brokers who have a contractual right to earn respectively commission and brokerage from the operation of a merchant vessel possess an insurable interest in that ship—*Buchanan v. Faber* (1899) 4 Com. Cas. 223; *O'Kane v. Jones* [2004] 1 Lloyd's Rep. 385. A buyer of goods on free on board terms will have an insurable interest in them from the time that they are at his risk under his purchase contract, because he has agreed to be responsible in the event of their loss during transit. The extent to which

1–49B

potential liability is a root of insurable interest is considered in paragraph 1–65 below.

Add to n.11:

1–64   *Dalby v. India & London Life Insurance Co* (1854) 15 C.B. 365.

Delete existing text and replace with the following:

1–65   **Risk of being held liable for damage to property.** It has been held that the supplier of components to be incorporated into a ship or industrial plant in the course of construction, acquires an insurable interest in the whole ship or plant by reason of the risk that he might become liable for its loss or damage if caused by defects in the product supplied by him, even though he has not agreed that it shall be at his risk and he has no legal interest in it— *Stone Vickers Ltd v. Appledore Ferguson Shipbuilders Ltd* [1991] 1 Lloyd's Rep. 288, 301; *National Oilwell (UK) Ltd v. Davy Offshore Ltd* [1993] 2 Lloyd's Rep. 582, 611; *Hopewell Project Management v. Ewbank Preece* [1998] 1 Lloyd's Rep. 448, 455. In the ninth and tenth editions of this work, these decisions were criticised on the grounds that they confused liability insurance with property insurance, that the possibility that the assured might become liable for negligently causing damage to another's property does not give him an insurable interest in that property, any more than an expectation of deriving a future benefit from it would do so, and that certain decisions were inconsistent with such a principle—see this numbered paragraph in the tenth edition. The reasoning in these cases has now been approved by a majority of the Court of Appeal in *Feasey v. Sun Life Assurance of Canada* [2003] 2 All E.R. (Comm) 587. The case held that the risk that the assured would be held liable to indemnify an employer of the lives insured, in the event that the latter was held liable to pay compensation for accidents occurring at their workplace, was a sufficient insurable interest to support an assurance on their lives and well-being, under which benefits were payable before liability had been established. The subcontractor cases are examined in paragraphs 1–155 to 1–159 below and the decision in *Feasey* is considered in paragraphs 1–93A to 1–93D below.

5. Insurable Interest in Lives

(a) *Principles of the 1774 Act*

Add to nn.41 and 42:

1–72   *Murphy v. Murphy* [2004] Lloyd's Rep I.R. 744, 751, *per* Chadwick L.J. In section 253 of the Civil Partnerships Act 2004, the presumption that one spouse has an unlimited interest in the life of the other has been extended to registered civil partners of the same sex.

(b) *Business and Status Relationships Between the Assured and the Life Assured*

Add the following new paragraphs:

Risk of potential liability. The life insurance cases so far considered, in which insurable interest was grounded in a liability arising on the death of the life insured, all involved a liability arising immediately upon the death. The question faced in *Feasey v. Sun Life Assurance Co of Canada* [2003] 2 All E.R. (Comm) 587 was whether it was sufficient on the death or injury of the lives insured, if the assured came under a potential but not certain liability to indemnify their employer for compensation payable to them or their dependents.   **1–93A**

In this case, the Steamship Mutual Underwriting Association (the Club) insured the liabilities of its members for personal injury or death sustained by crewmen and others on board their vessels. Until 1995 the Club had reinsured its liability to members under a conventional liability reinsurance policy at Lloyd's, but changes to insurance classification for reserving purposes made it more profitable for Lloyd's to reinsure the Club by means of a personal accident cover under which fixed benefits were payable rather than an indemnity against actual loss. Accordingly, the Syndicate granted a personal accident cover whereby benefits of fixed amounts were payable upon the death of, or injury to, a crewman or other person engaged to work on a member's vessel entered in the Club. The intention was to provide the Club with the approximate equivalent of an indemnity against their liabilities towards its members, taken over a three-year period. However, the individual benefits were payable to the Club upon the notification of the death or injury at a stage at which it was uncertain whether the relevant member was under a liability to pay compensation which entitled him to an indemnity from the Club. The Club was entitled to keep the benefit thus paid only when the liability of its member to pay compensation was in fact established in due course. This was therefore a personal accident insurance, paying out on the occurrence of death or injury to the lives insured, but performing the function of a liability reinsurance cover. The Syndicate reinsured its liability to the Club with Sun Life, and it was the latter's contention that the Club lacked an insurable interest in the lives and well-being of the crewmen, which gave rise to the litigation.   **1–93B**

By a majority the Court of Appeal affirmed the decision of Langley J. in the Commercial Court that the Club did have an insurable interest—[2002] 2 All E.R. (Comm) 492. The first point taken by Sun Life was that the Club could have no insurable interest in the lives insured, because it possessed no   **1–93C** legal or equitable interest in them, or, put another way, it had no legal relationship with them. The Court of Appeal held that life insurance did not require an assured to have a legal or equitable interest in the life assured or necessarily to be in a legal relationship with the life. It was sufficient if the assured would or might come under a liability towards a third party in the event of death or injury to the life, and there was no reason why a liability should not constitute a valid interest in a life. With respect, this is surely correct, as the decision in *Dalby v. India & London Life Insurance Co* demonstrates—see paragraph 1–49A above. The second point taken was that, because benefits were payable independently of whether the Club was liable to pay an indemnity in respect of an occurrence, no liability was incurred upon the contingency of death or injury, so that the death or injury merely gave rise to an expectation of loss, which was insufficient to support an insurable interest. This contention found favour with the dissenting member of the Court of Appeal, Ward L.J. The majority of the Court, Waller and Dyson L.JJ., rejected this argument, holding that in the case of this policy on many lives over a three-year period, during which time the assured was at risk of incurring liabilities in respect of accidents occurring to them, this potential liability constituted a valid insurable interest in the lives and well-being of the crewmen. They also drew support from decisions holding that sub-contractors possessed an insurable interest in plant under construction, by reason of their potential liability for damage which might result from their breach of legal duty—see paragraphs 1–155 to 1–159 below.

1–93D   It is submitted that the emphasis placed on differentiating this complex and carefully crafted policy from one on the life of a single named individual, does not produce a clear answer to the objection that the death or injury of a life assured obliged Syndicate 957 to pay the stipulated fixed benefit to the Club, although the casualty did not create of itself an automatic liability on the part of the Club towards its member, but only a potential liability depending on the circumstances of the death or injury. Be that as it may, it may be said that the death or injury of a crewman at least created a conditional liability on the part of the Club to pay for the member's legal defence and possibly to indemnify it against compensation, which it was liable to pay to its employee or his dependants. In the absence of authority to the contrary, it does not seem an unwarranted extension of the law to say that an assured who will come under a contingent liability towards A in the event of B being injured or killed, possesses a valid insurable interest in the life and health of B.

6. Insurable Interest in Property

(a) *Generally*

Add to n.28

Vendors and purchasers. The first sentence of the corresponding para-   **1–128**
graph in the 9th edition of this work was held in *Bestquest Ltd. v. Regency
Care Group Ltd.* [2003] Lloyd's Rep. I.R. 392 [21], to enunciate "an unex-
ceptionable proposition". In this case the buyer of a property, together with
the business run from it, was held to possess an insurable interest, not only
in the building but also in the income which would be at risk if the building
suffered fire damage in the interval between the date of exchange of contracts and the date for completion.

Add to n.50:

North British & Mercantile Ins. Co v. Moffat (1871) L.R. 7 C.P. 25, 30.   **1–133**

Delete existing paragraph and replace with the following:

Sub-contractors. It has been held in cases concerned with the right of an   **1–155**
insurer to sue an insured sub-contractor in the name of a co-assured, that
each sub-contractor engaged under a building or engineering contract is
entitled to insure the contract works for their full value and has an insurable
interest therein which enables him to claim on the policy for damage to a
part of the works, which is neither his property nor at his risk. In *Petrofina
(UK) Ltd v. Magnaload Ltd*—[1984] 1 Q.B. 127—a sub-contractor caused
damage to the contract works. He was one of several co-assureds on a
contractor's all risks policy on the works. The insurers indemnified the
employers for this damage. They then brought a subrogated claim for
damages for negligence against the sub-contractor responsible for the loss.
The latter argued that the claim could not be brought against it because it
was itself fully insured under the same policy in respect of the damaged
property. The policy provided that "the insured" were covered "against loss
of or damage to the insured property whilst at the contract site". The
"insured property" included:

> "The works and temporary works erected ... in performance of the
> insured contract and the materials ... for use in connection therewith
> belonging to the insured or for which they are responsible..."

Lloyd J. held, first, that as a matter of construction of the policy, each co-
assured was insured in respect of the entire contract works, including
property belonging to any other of the assureds or for which any other of
them was "responsible" in a general and non-legal sense. This led him to the

second question of whether the sub-contractor was entitled to recover the full value of all the insured property, despite having only a proprietary interest in just some of it, namely the equipment owned by him and being used to perform his sub-contract. Applying the analogy of the bailee entitled to insure goods entrusted to him for their full value, holding the amount in excess of his own interest in trust for their owners, Lloyd J. held that the positions of the bailee and sub-contractor were sufficiently close to entitle the latter to insure the entire works and to recover the whole of the insured loss, holding the excess in trust for his co-assureds—[1984] 1 Q.B. 127, 136.

The use of a single policy to cover all contractors' interests is no doubt commercially convenient, although the aim of protecting a sub-contractor from claims by insurers could be achieved by merely incorporating a waiver of subrogation clause in the policy or appropriate releases from liability to the employer and other contractors in the construction contract itself. It is difficult, however, to reconcile the learned judge's reasoning with other authorities. It had been established in *North British & Mercantile Insurance Co v. Moffatt* (1871) L.R. 7 C.P. 25 and *Engels v. Lancashire & General Assurance Co* (1925) Com Cas 202, that the description of insured property in a bailee's insurance as "goods in trust for which they are responsible" indicated that the insurers did not cover the proprietary interests of other persons in the goods insured, but rather the legal liability of the bailee to their owners. These cases were not cited to Lloyd J. and have been followed by the Court of Appeal in *Ramco v. International Insurance Co of Hannover* [2004] 2 All E.R. (Comm) 847, the Court doubting this part of the judgment in *Petrofina*. This point was first made by Birds in [1983] J.Bus.L. 497 and, it is submitted, destroys the analogy which the learned judge identified between the sub-contractor and a bailee who was entitled to insure goods for their full value. Even if the reference to responsibility had been absent, their positions were different. A bailee has a limited insurable interest in goods bailed to him, rooted in his possessory title to all of them and usually in addition in the rights and obligations created in the contract of bailment, whereas the sub-contractor had no legal or equitable interest in the insured property apart from his own equipment, so far as one may judge from the report. In those circumstances the decision might have been based on a finding that the insurers had impliedly waived the requirement of insurable interest, as they were free to do as the Life Assurance Act 1774 did not apply to this indemnity insurance on goods, as Lloyd J. held at page 136 of the report. The waiver might have been implied from the construction of the policy as one covering each sub-contractor in respect of the entire contract works, because no individual subcontractor could be expected to have a legal relationship to the entire insured property. (See paragraphs 1–16 and 1–40 above).

It should be noted that the decision is not an authority for the proposition that a potential liability for damage to property per se gives an assured an insurable interest in it.

Delete existing paragraph and replace with the following:

In *Stone Vickers Ltd v. Appledore Ferguson Shipbuilders Ltd* [1991] 1   **1–156**
Lloyd's Rep. 288 and *National Oilwell (UK) Ltd v. Davy Offshore Ltd* [1993]
2 Lloyd's Rep. 582, suppliers of components to marine construction sites
were held to have an insurable interest in the entire subject-matter under
construction, a ship and an off-shore oil production facility respectively, by
reason of their potential liability for causing damage to it through a fault in
the goods supplied by them. The test for the existence of an insurable
interest in the works was said to be whether the supplier might be materially
adversely affected by loss of or damage to the vessel or contract works by
reason of the incidence of any of the perils insured against by the policy in
question—[1993] 2 Lloyd's Rep. 582, 611. This seems to go beyond the
incidence of liability for causing damage to the contract works. At all events,
Colman J. held that insurable interest was created by a potential liability
arising from the existence of a contract between the assured sub-contractor
and the owner of property, or from the assured's proximate physical relationship to the property in question.

Apart from the *Petrofina* decision referred to above, Colman J. relied on
the decision of the Canadian Supreme Court in *Commonwealth Construction
Co v. Imperial Oil* 1976) 69 D.L.R. (3d) 558, in which it had been held that
sub-contractors in the mainstream of the construction activity have an
insurable interest in the contract works by reason of the real possibility of
being held liable for damage to the works or each other's property. However, it is difficult to see how the supplier of a component who did not
perform work on the construction site could be said to be in the mainstream
of the construction activity. In other cases, a security company and a firm of
consultant engineers have been held to fall outside it—*Canadian Pacific Ltd
v. Base Security Services Ltd* (1991) 77 D.L.R. (4th) 178; *Hopewell v. Ewbank
Preece* [1998] 1 Lloyd's Rep. 448. In this book we submitted that the
adoption of this test would lead to uncertainty in individual cases and also
criticised it on other grounds. The Court of Appeal in *Feasey v. Sun Life
Assurance of Canada* [2003] 2 All E.R. 587 has now approved it, stating that
there is no reason why the risk of being held liable for damage to property
should not support an insurable interest in it. We will return to it after
considering the decision of the Court of Appeal in another case relating to a
sub-contractor.

Delete existing paragraph and replace with the following:

In *Deepak Fertilisers & Petrochemicals Corporation v. ICI Chemicals &*   **1–157**
Polymers Ltd [1999] 1 Lloyd's Rep. 387, the litigation arose out of an
explosion at a methanol production plant in India in October 1992. The
plant had been built for Deepak between January 1988 and September 1991,
and was commissioned in October 1991. All construction work including
rectification was concluded by 11 August 1992. Another party to the action,

Davy McKee (London) Ltd ("Davy") provided technical and processing know-how to Deepak in connection with the construction and commissioning of the plant, the actual construction being performed by a third party. After the explosion Deepak claimed damages from Davy for negligence. One of Davy's defences was that the insurance arrangements in force disentitled Deepak from bringing its claim. The argument was that Davy was nominated as co-assured sub-contractor under the all-risks policy taken out by Deepak to insure the plant, that the action was in reality a subrogated action brought for the benefit of Deepak's insurers and that no claim could be brought against Davy as a co-assured itself entitled to be indemnified against loss and damage arising out of the explosion. This defence in turn raised the issue of whether Davy, as a sub-contractor providing services in connection with the construction of the plant, possessed an insurable interest in it at the time of the loss in October 1992.

Delete existing paragraph and replace with the following:

1–158   In the Commercial Court Rix J. rejected Deepak's submission that Davy possessed no insurable interest in the plant after the completion date. He said that he did not see why Davy did not have insurable interest in it as long as they were arguably responsible in some way for damage to it—[1998] 2 Lloyd's Rep. 139, 158. On appeal the situation was analysed differently. While the plant was under construction and Davy were working on it, Davy did possess an insurable interest in it because, if the plant was damaged or destroyed by any of the wide range of perils covered by the all-risks policy, such as fire or flood, they might lose the opportunity to perform their retainer and so earn their remuneration. In other words, they possessed a contractual right to payment, contingent upon the completion of the project. Once their work was completed, they would suffer financial loss from its damage or destruction only if that was caused by their own prior actionable breach of contractual or other legal duty. That was an appropriate subject-matter not for property insurance but rather for liability cover. Since the loss occurred after the completion date and after they had earned their money, they had by then ceased to be a co-assured with a valid insurable interest on the plant, so that the co-insurance provisions in their contract with Deepak afforded no defence to Deepak's claim—[1999] 1 Lloyd's Rep. 387, 399–400.

Delete existing paragraph and replace with the following:

1–159   In *Feasey v. Sun Life Assurance of Canada* [2003] 2 All E.R. (Comm) 587, the majority of the Court of Appeal noted that, although the court in *Deepak* had found an insurable interest in the contract works in the form of Davy's contractual right to remuneration upon completion, it did not disapprove of the decisions in *Stone Vickers* and *National Oilwell (UK)*. *Deepak* was not authority for the proposition that the insurable interest of liability could never be covered under property insurance. The court held that there was no reason why the risk of being held liable for causing damage to property should not create an insurable interest in the property so long as the assured was in a legal relationship to it and that liability was embraced in the description of the subject-matter of the insurance. A sub-contractor might well be able to satisfy those criteria depending on the wording of the policy on the contract works, but he would be unlikely to succeed if the policy was expressed to be simply on the plant. This does not mean that the risk of being held liable for causing damage to another person's property will by itself create an insurable interest in that property in every case—[2003] 2 All E.R. (Comm) 587, [95] per Waller L.J. Therefore, if a landowner permits another to place goods on his land but undertakes no legal responsibility for their safety and has no rights in or over them, the fact that he might become liable for causing damage to them does not create an insurable interest in the goods—*Macaura v. Northern Assurance Co* [1925] A.C. 619, 628, 630. By contrast, a sub-contractor will have a contract under which he is to perform duties in connection with the contractual works. The Court of Appeal did not approve the other criterion for an insurable interest identified in the *Stone Vickers* and *National Oilwell* cases, namely, that the assured's physical proximity to property would create an insurable interest in it.

(b) *Insurances Effected by the Assured on Behalf of Others*

In second paragraph, delete text after "... the insurers contended that they were not covered by the terms of the policy." and replace with the following:

"Goods held in trust for which they are responsible." The Court of   **1–182**
Common Pleas held that the assured were unable to recover because the teas had been resold by them before the fire and the purchasers had paid the purchase price, so that both property and risk in the goods had passed to the purchasers and they no longer had an insurable interest in them. The assured argued that even though they no longer had any responsibility for the teas, they were nonetheless goods held in trust and were therefore covered by the policy following *Waters v. Monarch Fire & Life Assurance Co* (1856) 5 E. & B. 870. The court distinguished *Waters*, in which the cover had not been restricted to goods for which the assured were responsible, and held that cover had been limited here to goods for which the assured were legally responsible. By limiting the cover in this way, the insurers were indicating that they did not intend to cover the proprietary interests of other persons interested in the goods. In effect the insurers were covering the legal liability of the assured, and in this case there was none. *Moffat* was followed by Roche J. in *Engel v. Lancashire & General Assurance Co* (1925) 30 Com. Cas. 202, and both decisions have been approved by the Court of Appeal in

15

Ramco v. International Insurance Co of Hannover [2004] 2 All E.R. (Comm) 847. In *Ramco*, the parties were in dispute as to the appropriate measure of indemnity in such a case. In the first instance Andrew Smith J. held that the assured should recover the full value of the goods, holding the surplus in excess of his own liability for their owner. The Court of Appeal did not need to decide the point, but said that they were "not necessarily satisfied" that this was correct. It is submitted that recovery should be limited to the amount for which a bailee is liable to owners of the bailed goods, because otherwise the purpose of the limitation of the insurers' liability would be frustrated and they would indirectly be indemnifying other persons with proprietary interests in the goods.

Add to n.36:

1–190   *O'Kane v. Jones* [2004] 1 Lloyd's Rep. 389, 408.

CHAPTER 7

PAYMENT OF PREMIUM

1. GENERAL RULES OF PAYMENT

Add to n.1:

Premium defined. This definition was approved and followed by Chief 7–2
Master Hurst in *Re Claims Direct Test Cases* [2003] Lloyd's Rep. I.R. 69, 75.

Add to n.84:

Liability for unpaid premium. In *Charman v. New Cap Reinsurance Corp.* 7–27
[2004] 1 All E.R. (Comm) 114, a cancellation clause provided that default in
payment of annual premium within 30 days of the due date was deemed to
be cancellation of the three-year reinsurance contract. It was assumed that
the marine usage set out in Marine Insurance Act 1906, s.53 applied to the
reinsurance so that the re-insured's default could not be established because
he was deemed to have paid it to the broker and the reinsurer's right of
recourse was against the broker. The issue of whether the custom applied
outside the marine market was left open.

CHAPTER 8

RETURN OF PREMIUM

1. GENERAL PRINCIPLES

Add new footnote 7a at the end of the second sentence:

Divisibility of risk.[7a] In *Swiss Reinsurance Co v. United India Insurance Co* **8–2**
[2005] Lloyd's Rep. I.R. 341 [53], Morison J. considered that it was, and that
the same question arose in relation to both marine and non-marine policies
namely, whether the consideration for the payment of premium was
apportionable. This was an issue of the way the insurance policy was con-
structed. In this case, a Construction All Risks reinsurance policy was held
to be one entire risk and the fact that the rate was calculated by pricing the
separate components of the risk individually and then producing a single
discounted premium, was not enough to make the risk divisible. Neither was
the fact that the policy provided cover for a first Construction Period and
then for a second Guarantee Maintenance Period, even if the second had not
incepted at the time that the reinsurers were discharged from liability by a
material change in the risk. The court went on to hold that the reinsurers
had in fact run a part of the risk under the second period of cover. No return
of premium was allowed.

3. OTHER MATTERS AFFECTING RETURN OF PREMIUM

Delete last sentence of this paragraph and replace as follows:

8-30   It is submitted that the courts are more likely to apply the marine rule by analogy in a non-marine context, on the grounds that insurance is a contract of utmost good faith and therefore especially unforgiving of fraud. However, the contrary view is that the Marine Insurance Act 1906, s.84(3)(a) is "an aberration as regards marine insurance"—MacDonald Eggers, Picken and Foss, *Good Faith and Insurance Contracts* (2nd ed. 2004) paragraph 16.43. See the special rules concerning fraud in the making of a claim— paragraphs 19–54 *et seq. post.* In *Swiss Reinsurance Co v. United India Insurance Co* [2005] Lloyd's Rep. I.R. 341 [55], Morison J. said that there was no reason why the section should not apply to non-marine insurance, but the above book was not cited to him.

CHAPTER 10

WARRANTIES AND OTHER POLICY TERMS

1. Classification of Terms

In the last sentence delete the word "perhaps". After n.43 in the second sentence, delete the words: "The Court was prepared to hold" and replace as follows:

"The Court was prepared to hold, *obiter*, ..."　　　　　　　　　**10–13**

Add to the end of the paragraph:

In the recent decision of the Court of Appeal in *Friends Provident Life &*　　**10–14**
Pensions Ltd v. Sirius International Insurance [2005] 2 All E.R. (Comm) 145,
a majority of the court disapproved the reasoning in the *McAlpine* case. An
issue arose concerning the consequences of the failure of the assured to
comply with a notice provision in a professional indemnity policy, which
required it to notify insurers of any claim made against it immediately, or of
circumstances which it became aware of which was likely to give rise to a
claim or loss. Notice was given some six years later to the particular insurers
in suit, who argued that, although not a condition precedent, the notice
clause was an intermediate term, breach of which, if sufficiently serious,
provided them with a defence to payment of the claim arising out of the un-
notified circumstances, even though it was not so serious as to entitle them
to terminate the contract for repudiatory breach. Noting that the reasoning
in *McAlpine* was *obiter*, Mance L.J. reviewed the subsequent authorities in
which it had been referred to and held that they were either decided at first
instance, did not apply it or did not involve argument as to its validity. He
could find no basis in law for introducing into insurance law a doctrine of

partial repudiatory breach, or for implying a term into the contract that insurers would be free from the liability to pay a claim in the event of a serious breach of the notice clause or a breach of it producing serious consequences. If insurance professionals in the market wanted to achieve that effect, then they must devise an appropriate wording to that end. Aldous L.J. delivered a short judgment agreeing with Mance L.J. Waller L.J. gave a dissenting judgment on this issue, upholding the conceptual validity of his own reasoning in *McAlpine*. The decision of the majority was followed in *Ronson International v. Patrick* [2005] 2 All E.R. (Comm) 453.

Add to n.55:

10–16   **The Unfair Terms in Consumer Contracts Regulations 1999.** The Regulations do not apply to the duty of good faith or any other duty imposed by law, as opposed to being created by an express contractual term—*Direct Life Insurance v. Khan* [2002] Lloyd's Rep. I.R. 364 [34–37].

Add to the end of the paragraph:

10–20   **Non-core terms in insurance policies.** In *Bankers Insurance Co Ltd v. Patrick South* [2004] Lloyd's Rep. I.R. 1, certain terms in a travel insurance policy, requiring prompt reporting of the full details of an incident which might give rise to a claim and the forwarding of legal process immediately upon receipt, were held to be unfair because they caused a significant imbalance in the parties' obligations to the assured's detriment. Cover was stated to be dependent upon the assured observing them and other terms of the policy. However, the court was concerned because the assured's breaches had caused prejudice to the insurer in this instance. Under Regulation 5 of the Regulations, an unfair term "shall not be binding on the consumer". However, Buckley J. held that it should be binding on the assured when his breach had caused prejudice to the insurer, a result which it is submitted is difficult to reconcile with the wording of the Regulation. He went on to hold that the assured's breaches of these innominate terms had occasioned sufficiently serious prejudice to the insurers to release them from liability to meet the claim under the principle of law enunciated in the *McAlpine* case— see paragraphs 10–13 to 10–14 *supra*.

2. WARRANTIES—DETAILED SURVEY

(a) *Definition and How Created*

Add to n.11:

Presumption of warranty. Followed and applied in *GE Reinsurance Corp.*   **10–30**
v. New Hampshire Ins. Co. [2004] Lloyd's Rep. I.R. 404 [48] [60]; *Toomey v. Banco Vitalicio de Espana* [2004] Lloyd's Rep. I.R. 354 [93–96]; [2005] Lloyd's Rep. I.R. 423 [40–42] (CA).

(e) *Waiver*

Add to n.42:

Waiver of breach of warranty. The decision of the Court of Appeal in   **10–104**
HIH Casualty & General Ins. Ltd v. Axa Corporate Solutions is now reported at [2002] 2 All E.R. (Comm) 1053, upholding the decision of the court below. The attempt to establish waiver of breach of warranty by promissory estoppel failed because the reinsurers did not realise that the breach of warranty had the possible consequence that the cover was wholly and absolutely discharged, and the reinsured was no better informed. A representor in this position is unlikely to make a clear representation that he is willing to forego the exercise of the right to treat himself as released from liability, and the representee is very unlikely to understand him to be saying so when he himself is unaware that there is a right available to be exercised, so that it will be difficult for him to demonstrate reliance on what was said or done.

CHAPTER 11

CONSTRUCTION OF POLICIES

1. ORDINARY MEANING OF WORDS

Add following new paragraphs after n.5:

General rules. The courts have made increasing reference in cases invol-   **11–1**
ving the construction of insurance policies to the general principles of
interpretation, restated in *Investors Compensation Scheme Ltd v. West
Bromwich Bldg. Soc.* (n.5), and it is clear that the exposition of the tradi-
tional canons of construction in this Chapter must now be read in the light
of these. In his speech, Lord Hoffmann summarised these principles as
follows:

"(1) Interpretation is the ascertainment of the meaning which a docu-
     ment would convey to a reasonable person having all the back-
     ground knowledge which would reasonably have been available to
     the parties in the situation in which they were at the time of the
     contract.
 (2) The background was famously referred to by Lord Wilberforce as
     the 'matrix of fact', but this phrase is, if anything, an understated
     description of what the background may include. Subject to the
     requirement that it should have been reasonably available to the
     parties and to the exception to be mentioned next, it includes
     absolutely everything which would have affected the way in which

25

the language of the document would have been understood by a reasonable man.

(3) The law excludes from the admissible background the previous negotiations of the parties and their declarations of subjective intent. They are admissible only in the action for rectification. The law makes this distinction for reasons of practical policy and, in this respect only, legal interpretation differs from the way we would interpret utterances in ordinary life ...

(4) The meaning which a document (or any other utterance) would convey to a reasonable man is not the same thing as the meaning of its words. The meaning of words is a matter of dictionaries and grammars; the meaning of the document is what the parties using those words against the relevant background would reasonably have understood them to mean. The background may not merely enable the reasonable man to choose between the possible meanings of words which are ambiguous but (even as occasionally happens in ordinary life) to conclude that the parties must, for whatever reason, have used the wrong words or syntax ...

(5) The 'rule' that words should be given their 'natural and ordinary meaning' reflects the commonsense proposition that we do not easily accept that people have made linguistic mistakes, particularly in formal documents. On the other hand, if one would nevertheless conclude from the background that something must have gone wrong with the language, the law does not require judges to attribute to the parties an intention which they plainly could not have had ... ."

In *Royal & Sun Alliance v. Dornoch* [2005] Lloyd's Rep. I.R. 544, Longmore L.J. commented on Lord Hoffmann's 4th principle and said at [16] that:

"there are dangers in judges deciding what the parties must have meant when they have not said what they meant for themselves. This is particularly dangerous when they have selected from the shelf or the precedent book a clause which turns out to be unsuitable for its purpose".

In *GE Reinsurance Corp. v. New Hampshire Ins. Co.* [2004] Lloyd's Rep. I.R. 404, at 412, Langley J. commented on Lord Hoffmann's 5th principle as follows:

"Although it is open to a court in limited circumstances ... to conclude that the words or syntax used is wrong, the purpose remains to construe the words used. I would add that in approaching the construction of a commercial document such as an insurance or reinsurance slip to which there may be several parties who became bound by its terms on separate occasions and following separate negotiations there is an added reason for caution before seeking to deduce an objective intention

26

which could result in ascribing a meaning to the words used other than the meaning they would normally bear".

As to recent insurance cases considering these principles, see in particular *Union Camp Chemicals Ltd v. ACE Ins. SA-NV* [2003] Lloyd's Rep. I.R. 487, *Canelhas Comercio Inportacao E Exportacao Ltd v. Wooldridge* [2004] Lloyd's Rep. I.R. 915 (described in paragraph 11–14, *post*), *McGeown v. Direct Travel Insurance* [2004] Lloyd's Rep. I.R. 599 and *Friends Provident Life and Pensions Ltd v. Sirius International Ins. Corp.* [2005] Lloyd's Rep. I.R. 135. In the last of these decisions, the background knowledge to be considered was the general practice of the insurance market in relation to the underwriting of professional indemnity risks (almost invariably written on a "claims made" basis) and the insuring of large risks by means of primary and excess layer policies (in the absence of any indication to the contrary, the scope of the excess layer is intended to be the same, apart from with regard to policy limits, as that provided under the primary layer).

Add to n.11:
    Sunport Shipping v. Tryg-Baltica International [2003] 1 All E.R. (Comm)   **11–3**
586, [27] and [56].

Add to n.19:

    Ordinary meaning. *Blackburn Rovers Football & Athletic Club Ltd v. Avon*   **11–6**
Insurance plc [2005] Lloyd's Rep. I.R. 447, 450.

Add to n.39:
    See also *Howells v. IGI Ins. Co. Ltd* [2003] Lloyd's Rep. I.R. 803.   **11–10**

2. Special Meanings of Words

Add new paragraph as follows:

    Departure from ordinary meaning of words. A term relating to a disease   **11–12**
that has a statutory and a medical meaning should be construed in accordance therewith: see *Cape plc v. Iron Trades Employers Ass. Ltd* [2004] Lloyd's Rep. 75, concerning the meaning of "mesothelioma" in an employer's liability policy.

Add new text after n.53 as follows:

11–14   In *Canelhas Comercio Importacao E Exportacao Ltd v. Wooldridge* [2004] Lloyd's Rep. I.R. 915, it was common ground that the decision in *Algemeene Bankvereeniging v. Langton* should be followed. In the context of a policy issued to cover risks in Brazil, the word "robbery" was to be understood not in any technical English legal sense, but in the sense in which ordinary commercial men would understand it. The Court of Appeal held further that detailed examination of the meaning of robbery under either English or Brazilian law was inappropriate. "The proper approach is to interpret the wording of the relevant clause as a whole in the context of the policy as a whole" (per Mance L.J. at paragraph 11), through the eyes of an ordinary commercial man. Having referred to the principles expressed by Lord Hoffmann in *Investors Compensation Scheme v. West Bromwich Bldg. Soc.* (see paragraph 11–1, *ante*), he continued:

> "It is of course true that one would expect any ordinary reasonable commercial person obtaining or issuing a policy such as the present to have a general conception of 'robbery' which one might also expect to correspond broadly with that used by legislators here and elsewhere. But a proper understanding ... requires consideration of how such a person would understand the whole clause in its context. That in turn involves considering the aim and purpose of the clause objectively ascertained from the language of the standard wording of this policy". (*ibid.* paragraph 12).

4. INCONSISTENCY AND AMBIGUITY

Add to end of paragraph as follows:

11–30   **Written and printed clauses.** This paragraph in the 9th edition was cited and the principle expounded therein applied in *Eurodale Manufacturing Ltd v. Ecclesiastical Insurance Office plc* [2003] Lloyd's Rep. I.R. 444, 449. The decision was upheld by the Court of Appeal: [2003] EWCA Civ 203.

Add to n.5 as follows:

11–31   **Printed clauses inapplicable.** Another example is *Royal & Sun Alliance Ins. Plc v. Dornoch* [2005] Lloyd's Rep. I.R. 544, in which a standard claims control clause suited to a property reinsurance was incorporated in a liability reinsurance cover. Longmore L.J. commented at [10] that, "[H]owever inapposite the clause may be, the court has to give it a sensible meaning in accordance with any helpful canons of construction which may be available".

Add following dictum to the end of the paragraph:

Ambiguity must be real.   11–35

"A court should be wary of starting its analysis by finding an ambiguity by reference to the words in question looked at on their own. And it should not, in any event, on such a finding, move straight to the *contra proferentem* rule without first looking at the context and, where appropriate, permissible aids to identifying the purpose of the commercial document of which the words form part. Too early recourse to the *contra proferentem* rule runs the danger of 'creating' an ambiguity where there is none..." (per Auld L.J. in *McGeown v. Direct Travel Insurance* [2004] Lloyd's Rep. I.R. 599, 603).

Add to the end of the paragraph as follows:

Terms in consumer insurance contracts. The only reported decision so far   11–36
to consider the Regulations in the context of an insurance policy, is *Bankers Ins. Co. Ltd v. South* [2004] Lloyd's Rep. I.R. 1. Strictly the case was considered under the earlier 1994 Regulations, but there are no material differences from the 1999 Regulations. Here a claim was made under the liability insurance section of a travel insurance policy in respect of the assured's potential liability arising from the use of a jet ski that he had hired. The insurers succeeded in their action for a declaration that they were not liable to indemnify the assured, Buckley J. accepting that a jet ski was a "motorised waterborne craft" within an exclusion clause. The exclusion was a core term. The phrase "motorised waterborne craft" would be understood by any reasonable assured as comprehending a jet ski and was therefore in plain intelligible language and therefore not subject to assessment for fairness. Even if it had been so subject, the term was not unfair in the circumstances of a relatively cheap travel insurance policy.

5. ADMISSIBILITY OF EXTRINSIC EVIDENCE

Add to n.53:

11–38   *Alliance Marine Aviation v. GE Frankona Reinsurance Ltd* [2005] Lloyd's Rep. I.R. 437, 445.

CHAPTER 12

RECTIFICATION

Add to n.13:

Evidence of common intention. *Thor Navigation Inc v. Ingosstrakh Insur-*   **12–5**
ance [2005] Lloyd's Rep. I.R. 490 [51].

Add to n.14:
Recently reported examples of the courts' refusal to allow rectification
include *Kiriacoulos Lines SA v. Compagnie d'Assurances Maritime Ariennes
et Terrestres* [2002] Lloyd's Rep. I.R. 795 and *Cape plc v. Iron Trades
Employers Ins. Ass. Ltd* [2004] Lloyd's Rep. I.R. 75.

Add to n.28:

Continuing common intention. The circumstances in which rectification   **12–10**
will be granted for this "unilateral mistake", where one party's mistake is
known to the other party, or where in exceptional cases the mistake is not
known but the other party behaves unconscionably, are set out in *Thor
Navigation Inc v. Ingosstrakh Insurance* [2005] Lloyd's Rep. I.R. 490 [57]–
[61]. In both cases the party resisting rectification is said to have failed to act
in accordance with generally accepted standards of commercial conduct.

CHAPTER 13

CONFLICT OF LAWS

1. JURISDICTION

Add to n.9:

Regulation 44/2001. See also the following recent insurance and reinsur-　**13–3**
ance cases concerning jurisdictional matters outside the scope of the Regulation—*Burrows v. Jamaica Private Power Co. Ltd* [2002] Lloyd's Rep. I.R.
466 (contract provided for jurisdiction in Jamaica); *Brotherton v. Aseguradora Colseguros SA* [2002] Lloyd's Rep. I.R. 848 (England the appropriate
forum for reinsurance of risks in Columbia under contract governed by
English law); *Lincoln National Life Ins. Co. v. Employers Reinsurance Corp.*
[2002] Lloyd's Rep. I.R. 853 (England the appropriate forum for reinsurance contract effected in the usual manner of the London market although
not all made in England); *Munchener Rucksversicherungs Gesselschaft v.
Commonwealth Ins. Co.* [2005] Lloyd's Rep. I.R. 97 and *Tonic Star Ltd v.
American Homes Ass. Co.* [2005] Lloyd's Rep. I.R. 32 (England the natural
forum for dispute over reinsurance contracts made in England on Lloyd's
market); *Royal & Sun Alliance Ins. plc v. Retail Brand Alliance Inc.* [2005]
Lloyd's Rep. I.R. 110 (New York the natural forum where assured had local
policy there and English master policy applicable only if no cover under
local policy); *Carvill America Inc. v. Camperdown U.K. Ltd* [2005] Lloyd's
Rep. I.R. 55 (England proper forum for claim for brokerage against reinsurers governed by English law); *Trygg Baltica Int. (U.K.) Ltd v. Boston
Compania de Seguros SA* [2005] Lloyd's Rep. I.R. 40 and *Markel International Ins. Co. Ltd v. La Republica Compania Argentina de Seguros* [2005]

Lloyd's Rep. I.R. 90 (England the appropriate forum for disputes on reinsurances effected in London on risks in Argentina); *Limit (No. 3) Ltd v.
PDV Ins. Co.* [2005] Lloyd's Rep. I.R. 552 (although reinsurance policy
governed by English law, action more appropriately tried in Venezuela
where parties, witnesses and documents based).

Add to the end of the paragraph as follows:

13–5   Although, in addition to those cited in footnote 16, a number of English
cases followed the decision in *Re Harrods (Buenos Aires) Ltd* (especially
American Motorists Ins. Co. v. Cellstar Corp. [2003] Lloyd's Rep. I.R. 294
and *Travelers Casualty and Surety Co. of Europe Ltd v. Sun Life Ass. Co. of
Canada (U.K.) Ltd* [2004] Lloyd's Rep. 846), a non-insurance case raising
the same issue— *Owusu v. Jackson* [2002] EWCA Civ 877, was referred to
the European Court of Justice, which has now ruled (Case C-281/02, March
1, 2005) that the Brussels Convention precludes a court of a Contracting
State from declining the jurisdiction conferred on it by Article 2 (see
paragraph 13–6, *post*), when the defendant is domiciled in England, on the
ground that a court of a non-Contracting State would be a more appropriate forum for the trial of the action, even if the jurisdiction of no other
Contracting State is in issue or the proceedings have no connecting factors
to any other Contracting State. Therefore, the decision in *Re Harrods
(Buenos Aires) Ltd* and the cases following it can no longer be regarded as
authoritative. Note, however, that in *Konkala Copper Mines plc v. Coromin*
[2005] EWHC 898 (Comm), Colman J. considered that the principle of
forum non conveniens would still apply in a case where the policy contained
an exclusive jurisdiction clause (see paragraph 13–13, *post*).

Add to n.59:

13–13   **Jurisdiction clauses.** In *Prifti v. Musini* [2004] Lloyd's Rep. I.R. 528, the
submission that an exclusive jurisdiction clause can be agreed by incorporation of standard terms containing one was rejected (at 533).

Add to n.60:

See also *Eviales SA v. SIAT* [2004] Lloyd's Rep. I.R. 187 and *Konkala
Copper Mines plc v. Coromin* [2005] EWHC 898 (Comm).

2. THE PROPER LAW OF THE CONTRACT

(a) *Proper Law: Common Law Principles*

Add to n.80:

Express choice of the proper law. In *King v. Brandywine Reinsurance Co.* **13–19**
[2005] 1 All E.R. (Comm) 1, the Court of Appeal did infer a choice of New
York law in a reinsurance dispute in part reliance on a "New York suable"
clause, reversing the decision of Colman J. ([2004] Lloyd's Rep. I.R. 554),
who had inferred English law from there having been a major placement in
London. New York arbitration was important, even though it depended on
a voluntary submission.

(b) *Proper Law: The Statutory Rules*

Add to n.10:

The Court of Appeal's decision in *American Motorists Ins. Co. v. Cellstar* **13–31**
Corp. [2003] Lloyd's Rep. 395, noting the decision at first instance, discussed
the issue without coming to a final answer. The case also concerned the issue
of jurisdiction and was referred to the European Court of Justice, whose
ruling on the issue (in *Owusu v. Jackson*) is mentioned in para.13–5, *ante*.

3. OTHER RELATED MATTERS

Add to n.2:

Proof of foreign law. See also *Eviales SA v. SIAT* [2004] Lloyd's Rep. I.R. **13–71**
187.

MISREPRESENTATION

(c) *Characteristics of Actionable Misrepresentation*

Add to the end of the paragraph:

Economides was followed in *Eagle Star Insurance Co. v. Games Video Co.* **16–13**
[2004] 1 All E.R. (Comm) 560, a case concerning the misrepresentation of
the value of a vessel to insurers. It was agreed by the parties and the judge in
reliance upon *Economides*, that value was a matter of opinion rather than
fact, so that a statement of value could amount to an actionable misrepresentation only if made in bad faith, and that there was no possibility of
an inquiry into whether there were reasonable grounds for the valuation.
The vessel was stated as being worth $1.8m, but was worth only $100–
$150,000. Forged and false documents were presented to insurers to support
the higher value, and Simon J. held that the assureds never entertained an
honest belief that the vessel was worth so much [118].

In *International Lottery Management v. Dumas* [2002] Lloyd's Rep. I.R.
237, a proposal form completed by an intending corporate assured, contained the question, "Have all documents necessary for legal operations in
the Host Country been obtained and are they currently valid?" The answer
given was "Yes". There was a declaration that the undersigned authorised
officer of the company declared that to the best of his knowledge the
answers given were true. It was submitted that the signatory honestly
believed that the above answer was correct, and that the form of the
declaration prevented any enquiry into its accuracy and whether the signatory had reasonable grounds for his belief. H.H. Judge Dean held that the
signatory had only a limited understanding of English, of the insurance

being sought and the purpose of the application form. He had not addressed his mind to what documents were needed. Had the answer been false, the declaration would not have saved the applicant because he could not entertain a genuine opinion on something about which he had not the least idea [63].

Add to the end of the second paragraph:

16–20   **Suppressio veri.** When an applicant for commercial insurance on property and business interruption was asked: "During the last 5 years, have you sustained any losses or had any claims made against you, whether or not insured. If 'YES', please state for each", he answered, "Yes", but gave no further details. In fact, he had sustained several losses, but his broker had only supplied the insurers with information on the one largest loss. Although literally correct, the answer was designed to mislead the insurers into thinking that there had been only one loss—*Stowers v. G A Bonus Plc* [2003] Lloyd's Rep. I.R. 402.

Add to the end of the paragraph:

16–33   By contrast, in *Stowers v. G A Bonus Plc* [2003] Lloyd's Rep. I.R. 402, where an applicant was asked to say whether he had experienced any losses in the last five years, and if so to give details, he answered "Yes", but gave no details. This was literally true, because he had sustained several losses in that time. It was argued that the insurers had waived further disclosure by failing to ask for details. However, his broker had supplied the insurers with details of the one largest loss, and they were entitled to believe that this information constituted the relevant missing details, and so were unaware that there had not been full disclosure.

Add to the end of the paragraph:

16–53   **Leaders and followers.** Another answer to the problem is for the following insurers to give evidence that when the broker approached them, they were influenced by the fact that a respected leader had subscribed the slip, and relied on his judgement in following him, assuming that he had been given a fair presentation of the risk. Where this evidence is accepted, the court may well hold that, in order to make a fair presentation to them, the broker should have disclosed the material fact that the presentation to the leader had been unfair and incorrect, and his failure to do so had induced them to subscribe, so that they are entitled to avoid. Alternatively, it may be held that the broker impliedly represented that a fair presentation had been made to the leader, when it had not, and that this was relied upon by the following market. This approach has been followed in *Aneco v. Johnson & Higgins*

[1998] 1 Lloyd's Rep. 565; *International Lottery Management v. Dumas* [2002] Lloyd's Rep. I.R. 237 and *International Management Group v. Simmonds* [2004] Lloyd's Rep. I.R. 247. It does not represent a rule of law, but depends upon the evidence of the followers' reliance on the leader's judgement and expertise being accepted by the court.

n.77:

Exclusion of insurers' remedies for misrepresentation. Delete "[2001] 2 **16–59** Lloyd's Rep. 483 (under appeal to the House of Lords at the time of writing)" and substitute with "[2003] 1 All E.R. (Comm) 349", and delete "*HIH Casualty & General Ins. Ltd v. New Hampshire Ins. Co* [2001] 2 All E.R. (Comm) 39, 94–95."

After n.78, delete the word "secondly". Delete text between nn.77 and 78 and replace with the following:

For reasons of public policy, the law will not enforce a clause which purports to protect the assured from the consequences of his own fraudulent misrepresentations, because no-one should be permitted to benefit from his own wilful wrongdoing—*HIH Casualty & General Ins. Ltd v. Chase Manhattan Bank* [2003] 1 All E.R. (Comm) 349,[16],[68]. In that case, the House of Lords left the question open of whether a clearly worded clause can remove the right of an insurer to avoid the insurance or to hold the assured liable in damages, in the event of a fraudulent misrepresentation by the assured's agent to make the contract of insurance. The clause in question did not on its true construction exclude the insurer's remedies for fraud by the agent.

GOOD FAITH AND THE DUTY OF DISCLOSURE

(a) *Duty of Utmost Good Faith*

Add to n.1:

For a detailed survey of the application of the principle of utmost good   **17–1**
faith to insurance contracts, see MacDonald Eggers, Picken and Foss, *Good
Faith and Insurance Contracts* (2nd ed., 2004).

Delete text in n.7 and replace as follows:

ibid. citing *Cox v. Bankside Agency Ltd* [1995] 2 Lloyd's Rep. 437, 462.   **17–2**
Other examples concerning the discretion of insurers to settle proceedings
against their assured are *Groom v. Crocker* [1939] 1 K.B. 194, 203 and
Beacon Insurance Co v. Langdale [1939] 4 All E.R. 204, 206. Other instances
may be the duty of the assured to have regard to the interests of the insurer
when taking action against a third party who has caused an insured loss—
see paras.22–41 to 22–42, *post* and the duty of a reinsurer to exercise his
powers under a claims control clause in good faith and not capriciously or
arbitrarily—*Eagle Star Ins. Co. v. Cresswell* [2004] Lloyd's Rep. I.R. 537
[55].

(c) *Duty of the Assured*

Add to the end of the paragraph:

17–17   **Effect of questions in proposal form.** The questions may also show that the insurers regard certain matters as important to them, and worthy of disclosure. For instance, in *Hazel v. Whitlam* [2005] Lloyd's Rep. I.R. 168, [25–27] the proposer's occupation was material to the particular motor insurers, because they specialised in offering low rates and therefore excluded certain higher risk occupations. The proposal form required the proposer to state his occupation and nature of business—both full and part time—and to give his employer's or business address. The answers given, after amendments by the broker, were: "shop assistant retailing", "Worthing Road, Horsham" and therefore did not mention that he was a trainee golf professional, working in a sports shop connected to a nine hole golf course. Had those details been stated, the insurers would not have accepted the risk, and they were entitled to avoid the policy. It is unclear whether the inclusion of a question about a particular subject-matter makes it material for purposes of the law of misrepresentation and non-disclosure, even when it would not have influenced a prudent underwriter in reaching a decision about the proposed risk, or whether the intending assured's obligation to answer the question correctly rests on some other basis. The case-law is discussed in paragraph 17–39 below. It should also be noted that in *Hazel*, the assured's broker was aware of the importance attached by insurers to the occupation of an intending assured although the assured was not, and it seems to have been tacitly accepted by the Court of Appeal, that it was objectively material to an insurer offering low cost motor insurance.

Add to n.53:

17–19   This paragraph in the current edition was endorsed by the Court of Appeal in *Doheny v. New India Assurance Co* [2005] All E.R. (Comm) 382, in which it was held *obiter* that, if a question was to be interpreted as confined to whether individual applicants had ever been declared bankrupt, the insurers had waived disclosure of the insolvency of companies of which they had been directors. Another case in which nice distinctions were made is *Pedley v. Avon Insurance Co* [2003] EWHC 2007 (QB) where a proposal form asked: "Have you, or any person connected with the ownership or management of the business ever been declared bankrupt?" The proposer replied "No". Pedley's husband had carried on the same sort of business at the same premises until he had been declared bankrupt, and he was an employee of the new business of which she was proprietor. H.H. Judge Hegarty Q.C. held that the insurers had not established non-disclosure, because there had been a gap between the closure of the husband's business and the opening of his wife's, so that they were not the same business despite having the same name and he was an employee, not a proprietor of the firm. Another question was: "Have you ever suffered loss or incurred liability in the last three years?" Answer: "No". The husband's business had in fact sustained numerous undisclosed losses, but this answer was correct because the word "your" in the question, limited disclosure to the wife's business.

Add to n.67:

Duration of duty of disclosure. When a reinsurance was made in advance   **17–22** of the underlying insurance, constituting a standing offer of reinsurance which was accepted by primary assureds agreeing to be reinsured, the time for disclosure of material facts by the assured ran until the time of acceptance, so that news of a US$20m loss received by an assured just after acceptance did not have to be disclosed—*Bonner v. Cox Dedicated Corporate Member Ltd* [2005] Lloyd's Rep IR 569.

Delete existing paragraph and replace with following paragraphs:

Inducement. To succeed in a defence of non-disclosure, the insurer must   **17–28** prove not only that the assured failed to disclose a material fact but that the non-disclosure induced the making of the contract—*Pan Atlantic Ins. Co. v. Pine Top Ins. Co.* [1995] A.C. 501, 549. This means that the non-disclosure must have been an effective cause of the underwriter making the contract which he did, but need not have been the sole cause of this—*Assicurazioni Generali SpA v. ARIG* [2003] 1 All E.R. (Comm) 140 [59] [87]. To prove this, the insurer must establish that had he known the undisclosed fact, he would not have concluded the contract on the same terms or at all, because if he would have made the same contract, the non-disclosure cannot have made any difference—*Assicurazioni Generali In. Co. v. ARIG, supra; St Paul Fire & Marine Ins. Co. v. McConnell Dowell Constructors* [1995] 2 Lloyd's Rep. 116,124–125; *Marc Rich v. Portman* [1997] 1 Lloyd's Rep. 225,234–235; *Ins. Co. of the Channel Islands v. Royal Hotel* [1998] Lloyd's Rep. I.R. 154,158. It is sufficient if disclosure of the relevant fact would have led the underwriter to ask further questions which, if answered correctly, would have led him to impose different terms—*International Management Group v. Simmonds* [2004] Lloyd's Rep. I.R. 247 [145]. However, in *Drake Ins. Plc v. Provident Ins. Plc* [2004] Q.B. 601, it was held that, if the assured had disclosed a prior speeding conviction on renewal of his motor policy, the reclassification of an earlier accident as a "no fault" accident would have come to light, so that no increased premium would have been chargeable, and the motor insurer failed to establish inducement [62–64] [135]. Where a court claim for $5 million was pending at the time of placement but was not disclosed to liability insurers, the fact that the assured's loss record was fundamental to assessment of the premium, and the premium would therefore have been raised, was sufficient to establish inducement, even if the precise amount of the increase was not established—*New Hampshire Ins. Co. v. Oil Refineries Ltd.* [2003] Lloyd's Rep. I.R. 386.

17–28A   There is no legal presumption that an underwriter is induced to enter into a contract by non-disclosure of a material fact, but if the fact is obviously material it may justify the court in inferring that an underwriter was induced to contract even where he does not give evidence to the court, especially where the evidence is accepted that other underwriters on the same risk were induced to contract—*Assicurazioni Generali Ins. Co. v. ARIG* [2003] 1 All E.R. (Comm) 140, [62], following *St Paul Fire & Marine Ins. Co. v. McConnell Dowell Constructors* [1995] 2 Lloyd's Rep. 116–117—although of course, the assured may call evidence to rebut the inference—*Gaelic Assignments v. Sharp* 2001 S.L.T. 914, 918. Cases where a court is prepared to draw such inference, are invariably those where other underwriters' evidence has been accepted—*Rich v. Portman* [1996] 1 Lloyd's Rep. 430, 440–442; *Sirius Ins. Corp. v. Oriental Ass. Corp.* [1999] Lloyd's Rep. I.R. 343, 351; *Aneco v. Johnson & Higgins* [1998] Lloyd's Rep. 565, 597; *International Management Group v. Simmonds* [2004] Lloyd's Rep. I.R. 247, [149]; *Toomey v. Banco Vitalicio Espana* [2004] Lloyd's Rep. I.R. 354 [73–74] (misrepresentation) not challenged on appeal [2005] Lloyd's Rep. I.R. 423. These cases show that the inference may be drawn even when the insurer has not done everything possible to secure the attendance of the absent underwriter in order to give evidence in court, such as issuing a subpoena. The readiness of the courts to infer inducement in this kind of case has been criticised on the grounds that it allows an imprudent or uncooperative underwriter, whose testimony might be unfavourable, to shelter behind that of his more prudent co-subscribers— Yeo, Of Inducement and Non-Disclosure in Insurance Contracts [2004] 10 J.I.M.L. 84.

It is sometimes the case that following underwriters are induced to subscribe to the risk more by the fact that a respected leading underwriter with experience of the class of insurance involved has subscribed to the slip before it was shown to them than by the information which was not disclosed to them. In such a case the fact that the broker failed to make a fair presentation to the leader, if proved, is itself a material fact which should have been disclosed to them, and they are entitled to avoid the cover for the broker's failure to do so—*International Management Group v. Simmonds* [2004] Lloyd's Rep. I.R. 247 [150–151] and authorities there cited.

The court is reluctant to allow the assured to refer back to risks previously underwritten by the underwriter for other assureds, because of the potentially oppressive disclosure of confidential documents involved and the difficulty of assessing the relevance of how other risks of a different overall complexion were handled. It does not necessarily follow that an underwriter acting carelessly and imprudently would have agreed the same terms if his mind had been directed to an obviously material fact—*Rich v. Portman* [1996] 1 Lloyd's Rep. 430, 440–442—but where the underwriter found the business commercially attractive he may well have accepted the risk on the same terms despite full disclosure—*Kingscroft Ins. Co. v. Nissan Fire & Marine Ins. Co.* [1999] Lloyd's Rep. I.R. 603, 631; *Glencore International AG v. Alpina Ins. Co Ltd* [2004] 1 All E.R. (Comm) 766 [76]. Where an underwriter relied upon a favourable albeit incorrect interpretation of an exclusion clause in the proposed policy, and accordingly would have attached little importance to certain material facts if they had been disclosed to him, he did not establish inducement—*Kausar v. Eagle Star Ins. Co.* [2000] Lloyd's Rep. I.R. 154.

Add to n.90:
   Mackender v. Feldia is reported at [1967] 2 Q.B. 590.   **17–29**

Add new paragraph as follows:

   Avoidance is effective once declared. The insurer's declaration that the   **17–29A**
insurance is avoided for non-disclosure does not require the intervention of the court in order to become effective. The contract is avoided from the moment that the insurer's election to avoid it is communicated to the assured—*Brotherton v. Aseguradora Colseguros* [2003] 1 All E.R. (Comm) 774; [2003] 2 All E.R. (Comm) 298, 311–312,316; *Drake Insurance Plc v. Provident Insurance Plc* [2003] 1 All E.R. (Comm) 759,768. These decisions treat avoidance and rescission as the same in this respect, despite the likely common law origins of the former and the equitable origins of the latter. Be that as it may, it seems plain that, if the insurer's election to avoid is challenged by the assured but later upheld by the court, there is no need for the court to pronounce a decree of rescission or avoidance. A simple declaration that the insurer was entitled to avoid the contract is enough. "Rescission is an act of the party, effective as soon as made, and regarded by the courts as so effective provided that the appropriate circumstances for rescission existed at that time"—*Brotherton v. Aseguradoras Colseguros* [2003] 2 All E.R. (Comm) 298, 316 *per* Buxton L.J.

Delete existing text and replace as follows:
   The doctrine of avoidance *ab initio* can produce unexpected consequences   **17–31**
if the contract is to be treated as never having existed. In *Commercial Union v. Mander* [1996] 2 Lloyd's Rep. 640, a reinsurer resisted a claim by the reinsured on the alternative grounds of non-disclosure and failure to settle the assured's claim in a businesslike manner. In order to defeat a claim of legal privilege raised by the reinsured to resist production of documents relating to the settlement of the claim, the reinsurer asserted a common interest privilege in them. The court held that common interest privilege could have been claimed, but for the reinsurer's claim to be entitled to avoid

the reinsurance contract. Since the reinsurer was contending that the reinsurance contract never existed, it could not at the same time rely on its existence at the time that the reinsured acquired the privileged documents in order to establish a common interest in them. A similar point has arisen where an insurer or reinsurer has claimed not to be bound by an exclusive jurisdiction clause because a declaration of avoidance, although contested, had resulted in the entire contract, including the clause, ceasing to exist and being deemed never to have existed. In the Australian case of *FAI v. Ocean Marine Mutual* [1998] Lloyd's Rep. I.R. 24 (NSW Comm. Div.), it was held that the argument failed because the contract did not just "fall away" as soon as the reinsurer declared it avoided, but only if a competent tribunal pronounced a decree of rescission. The words *ab initio* should not be taken literally. Avoidance *ab initio* just meant that the parties were to be restored substantially to the position they would have been in if no contract had been concluded, but the fact remained that there was a contract. Similar conclusions were expressed by the Canadian courts in *Ash v. Corporation of Lloyd's* (1992) 9 O.R. (3d) 755 (CA Ont.) and *Morrison v. Society of Lloyd's* (2000) 224 N.B.R. (2d) 1. It is submitted that *Mackender v. Feldia* [1967] 2 Q.B. 590 is also authority for the proposition that the contract is not to be treated as never having existed. At page 603 Diplock L.J. said:

> "[W]hen what is said to be a "voidable" contract is said to be "avoided", that does not mean that the contract never existed but that it ceases to exist from the moment of avoidance, and that upon its ceasing there may then arise consequential rights in respect of things done in performance of it while it did exist which may have the effect of undoing those things as far as possible".

This remains a difficult decision in so far as it seems to support the notion of prospective as opposed to retrospective cancellation, and the Court's decision that the parties remained bound by a Belgian exclusive jurisdiction clause may nonetheless have to be explained by reference to the principle of autonomy of arbitration and jurisdiction clauses, although that was not the basis on which judgment was given.

(d) *Materiality*

At line 8, delete text after "this seems to contradict the established criterion for materiality" and replace with the following:

17–39 **Opinion of particular insurer.** There is some authority for the proposition that the duty to act in the utmost good faith obliges the assured to disclose facts which he knows are regarded as material by the particular insurer, because to conceal such matters would be a breach of that duty even if they would not be generally regarded as material to a prudent insurer. Thus, in *Cantieri Meccanico Brindisino v. Janson* [1912] 3 K.B. 452, 463, Vaughan-Williams L.J. remarked that in marine insurance, a party might well be obliged to disclose facts under the Marine Insurance Act, section 17, which imposes the general duty to act in good faith, although he might not be obliged to do so by section 18 of the Act, which contains the detailed rules concerning communication of material facts. More recently in *CTI v. Oceanus* [1984] 1 Lloyd's Rep. 476, 512, Parker L.J. said *obiter* that, if the insurer shows interest in circumstances which are not material within section 18 of that Act, section 17 requires the assured to disclose them fully and fairly. In the non-marine case of *McNealey v. Pennine Insurance* [1978] 2 Lloyd's Rep.18, 20, Lord Denning M.R. put it differently without reference to section 17 of the Act and said that, "All facts are material which are, to the knowledge of the proposed assured, regarded by the insurers as material: and that extends to the knowledge of his broker also".

The authorities said to support these propositions are discussed in *Good Faith and Insurance Contracts* by MacDonald Eggers, Picken & Foss (2nd ed., 2004) at pages 226–229. It is submitted that on closer examination they do not constitute binding authority for them. All the pronouncements cited appear to be *obiter dicta*. In some instances the court had already found the fact in issue to be objectively material, as in H*arrower v. Hutchinson* (1870) L.R. 5 Q.B. 584, 594, and in the *McNealey* case cited above where it was actually common ground between the parties that the assured should have disclosed his occupation. The recent case of *Hazel v. Whitlam* [2005] Lloyd's Rep. I.R. 168, cited at paragraph 17–17 above, also seems to be a case where the court considered the occupation of the assured to be objectively material to the prudent insurer offering low cost motor insurance. In many instances the assured's answers to questions in the proposal form were warranted to be correct by a "basis of the contract" clause so that the question of their materiality did not arise, as in *Glicksman v. Lancs. & General Assurance* [1925] 2 K.B. 593, 609 and [1927] A.C. 139, 143–144; *Keeling v. Pearl Assurance* [1923] 129 L.T. 573, 575; *Hair v. Prudential Assurance* [1983] 2 Lloyd's Rep. 667, 673. In other instances it is doubtful whether the court was dealing with the point at all, such as in *Schoolman v. Hall* [1951] 1 Lloyd's Rep. 139, 144, and *Roberts v. Plaisted* [1989] 2 Lloyd's Rep. 341, 345. In *The Bedouin* [1894] P. 1, 12, Lord Esher appears to have endorsed the more limited proposition that the assured must give honest answers to questions asked by the insurer. *Arnould on Marine Insurance* supports this on the basis that a fraudulent misrepresentation does not have to be material in order to be actionable—(16th ed., 1997) Vol. 3, para. 671. (*Sed quaere* in view of section 20 (4) of the Marine Insurance Act 1906).

On the other hand, the proposition that the inclusion of a question in a proposal form made its subject-matter material, was expressly rejected by the Privy Council in *Mutual Life Insurance v. Ontario Metal Products* [1925] A.C. 344. This decision was followed in *Babatsikos v. Car Owners' Mutual*

[1970] 2 Lloyd's Rep. 314, 322, and it was cited with approval by Lord Mustill in *Pan Atlantic Insurance v. Pine Top Insurance* [1995] A.C. 501, 539–541, including the passage in the judgment in which it was held that asking questions did not in itself make their subject-matter material. We submit that the assured is not obliged to volunteer information of circumstances which are not objectively material within section18 of the Act, even if he or his broker knows that the particular insurer thinks that they matter. It is open to a court to hold that his duty to act in good faith obliges him to be truthful when he chooses to give answers to questions asked of him, in the knowledge that the insurer will rely on the answers given, following the *dicta* of Parker L.J. in *CTI v. Oceanus,* cited above.

Add to n.38:

17–45   **Information and opinions.** *Strive Shipping Corp. v. Hellenic Mutual War Risks Association* [2002] 1 All E.R. (Comm) 213, 274, citing the judgment of Gibbs C.J. in *Durrell v. Bederley* (1816) Holt N.P. 283, 285 stating, "Loose rumours which have gathered together, no-one knows how, need not be communicated. Intelligence, properly so called, and as it is understood by mercantile men, ought to be disclosed when known". In a modern context, newspaper reports bearing on the risk must attain the level of credible intelligence and not be merely idle gossip if they are to be material— *Brotherton v. Aseguradora Colseguros* [2003] 2 All E.R. (Comm) 298, 302. A similar rule applies to anecdotal and imprecise reports of a loss which would be material to the proposed insurance—*Bonner v. Cox Dedicated Corporate Member Ltd.* [2005] Lloyd's Rep. I.R. 569. However, once the report or rumour passes the credibility threshold and becomes information which would influence a prudent underwriter, it should be disclosed even if the assured is satisfied that it is incorrect—*International Management Group v. Simmonds* [2004] Lloyd's Rep. 247, 273. No doubt the assured would at the same time disclose his own reasons for disbelieving it.

Add at the end of the paragraph:

17–51   In liability insurance and reinsurance details of the assured's or reinsured's loss record are invariably material circumstances and should be disclosed, since they are usually fundamental to a prudent underwriter's assessment of the risk and his calculation of the premium—*New Hampshire Ins. Co. v. Oil Refineries Ltd.* [2003] Lloyd's Rep. I.R. 386.

Add to n.90:

17–56   **Previous convictions.** Some motor insurers operate a fixed "points" system, in which every motoring conviction and accident in the five years prior to a proposal disclosed by the assured carries a preset points rating. The total number of points accumulated over a certain level triggers a rise in premium or declinature depending on the amount. This enables approved brokers to accept or reject a proposal and, where accepted, to calculate the assured's premium without recourse to the insurer. In *Drake Insurance Plc v. Provident Insurance Plc* [2004] Q.B. 601, it was common ground that a speeding conviction was a material fact and should be disclosed to such an insurer via the approved broker. However, Clarke L.J. left for further consideration [140–142] the question of whether it was material if the points which were to be added in consequence were counterbalanced by the deduction of points brought about by the assured establishing that a third party was responsible for an accident previously notified to the insurer. In such a case, materiality could be said to depend upon the significance of the conviction to a notional prudent motor insurer using a fixed points formula, and the speeding conviction would not be material to him in those circumstances. Rix L.J. also questioned why the hypothetical question of what would have been the reaction of a prudent underwriter if disclosure of the speeding conviction had been made, should be answered on the incorrect assumption that the status of the accident remained unaltered [73–78]. If it is right to assume that the assured would have disclosed not only the conviction but also the settlement by the third party, then the speeding conviction would not have been material because it could not have triggered a re-rating.

Add to the end of the paragraph, after n.3:

If an assured has been convicted of a crime prior to placement, but does not disclose the conviction because he is convinced that he was the victim of a miscarriage of justice, the insurer is entitled to avoid the insurance on discovering the conviction, assuming that the tests of materiality and inducement are satisfied, even if the assured at that stage possessed the evidence to prove his innocence if allowed to do so—*March Cabaret & Casino Ltd v. The London Assurance* [1975] 1 Lloyd's Rep. 169, 177; *Brotherton v. Aseguradora Colseguros* [2003] 2 All E.R. (Comm) 289 [23], disagreeing with Colman J. in *Strive Shipping Corp. v. Hellenic Mutual War Risks Association, The "Grecia Express"* [2002] 2 All E.R. (Comm) 213, 272. Materiality is to be tested at the time of placement and not by reference to subsequent events.

Delete existing paragraph and replace as follows:

Allegation of criminal offences. Is a proposer for insurance obliged to **17–58** disclose that he has been charged with a criminal or disciplinary offence which itself would be material to the risk if he had in truth committed it? If the charge is dropped or he is acquitted prior to conclusion of the insurance, then it need not be disclosed—*Reynolds v. Phoenix Ass. Co.* [1978] 2 Lloyd's Rep. 440. If the assured knows despite having been acquitted that he was, in reality, guilty of the offence, then his guilt should be disclosed—*March Cabaret Club & Casino v. The London Assurance* [1975] 1 Lloyd's Rep. 169, 177; *Strive Shipping Corp. v. Hellenic Mutual War Risks Association, The "Grecia Express"* [2002] 2 All E.R. (Comm) 213, 271; *Brotherton v. Aseguradora Colseguros* 289, 309.

The courts have reached different conclusions about disclosure of the allegation when the assured denies his guilt, and the matter remains unresolved at the time the insurance is concluded. In *Reynolds* it was held that the assured need not disclose an allegation which he knew to be baseless, but if he knew it to be true it was the commission of the offence which should be disclosed. In the New Zealand case of *Gate v. Sun Alliance Insurance Ltd* [1995] L.R.L.R. 385, 408 (NZ High Court), it was said that materiality should depend upon whether the assured was subsequently acquitted or convicted of the alleged offence, so that in effect it was the commission of an offence which should have been disclosed. By contrast, in *March* and in *Inversiones Manria SA v. Sphere Drake Insurance Co Plc, The "Dora"* [1989] 1 Lloyd's Rep. 69, it was held that insurers were entitled to be told about matters which raised doubts about the risk, as well as those which increased it, that the materiality of an allegation had to be tested at the time of placement and not by reference to subsequent events and that an allegation which would affect the mind of a prudent insurer was a material fact and should be disclosed.

More recent authorities have upheld the approach in the *March* and *Dora* decisions. In *Strive Shipping Corp. v. Hellenic Mutual War Risks Association, The "Grecia Express"*, [2002] 2 All E.R. (Comm) 213, Colman J. held that an allegation which would affect the judgment of a prudent insurer was itself a material fact which should be disclosed, and the fact that it was unfounded did not divest it of materiality. The right course was to disclose the allegation and the assured's reasons for denying his guilt, so that the insurer could make up his own mind. In *Brotherton v. Aseguradora Colseguros* [2003] 2 All E.R. (Comm) 298, reinsurers sought declarations that they were entitled to avoid reinsurance contracts, which reinsured Columbian insurance companies against losses under bankers' blanket bond and professional indemnity policies granted to a Columbian bank. The cover included losses caused by dishonest and fraudulent acts of the bank's employees. The ground of avoidance was the non-disclosure by the reinsureds of reports in the Columbian press of (1) allegations of criminal activity in the conduct of the bank's business and serious misconduct by the bank's president and (2) investigations commenced by the Columbian authorities concerning the truth of such allegations involving disciplinary charges against him. The reinsureds appealed against an order striking out averments in their pleadings that the allegations were politically motivated and without foundation, and which would have resulted in the court having to try not only the issue of whether the press allegations were material on their own, but whether the allegations reported were well-founded. They argued that the only circumstances which had to be disclosed were existing facts, so that allegations of possible misconduct were immaterial unless shown to be based on hard fact.

The Court of Appeal dismissed the appeal, stating that circumstances incapable of proof had sometimes to be disclosed. One example was the existence of intelligence concerning the possible loss of or damage to the thing insured, discussed in paragraph 17–45 above. Another was an allegation that an offence had been committed by the assured. The Court approved the statements in the *March* and *Dora* cases that an assured should disclose an allegation or charge that he was guilty of a criminal offence, even when he knew them to be baseless. The Court added that issues of materiality and inducement would fall to be determined on the basis that, if there had been disclosure, it would have embraced all aspects of the assured's knowledge and evidence to support his statement that he was innocent of the charges. Two principles supported this conclusion. (1) "The sound philosophical basis of the duty of disclosure in an insurance context is that a true and fair agreement for the transfer of risk on an appropriate basis depends on equality of information", *per* Mance L.J. at [24]. (2) An enquiry *ex post facto* into the correctness of the allegation in question would necessitate a long, costly and probably inconclusive public enquiry or trial. "That would seem to be a complete departure from the important requirement of certainty in insurance dealings", *per* Buxton L.J. at [41].

Add at the end of the paragraph:

Dishonest conduct. In *Markel International Insurance Co v. La Republica*   **17–59**
Cia. Argentina de Seguros [2005] Lloyd's Rep. I.R. 90, the misconduct of a reinsured's producing broker was held capable of being a material fact. As a matter of common sense, a dishonest broker who was anxious to place a risk and therefore earn his commission would perhaps misrepresent facts or suppress information more readily. In this case, the misconduct alleged was that the broker had left the London Market some three years before the placement after he had misled a leading underwriter about reinsurance security that he wrongly claimed to have obtained for the latter's Syndicate. It was also held that "premium skimming", charging almost twice as much premium to the primary insurer as had been charged by the reinsurer, was arguably material and disclosable where the slips had been incorrectly entered up to disguise both this fact and the commission being charged by the broker.

Add to n.24:

17–62   **Prior refusals.** *Stowers v. GA Bonus Plc* [2003] Lloyd's Rep. I.R. 402, 410, where a previous insurer had declined to invite renewal of a combined commercial insurance policy granted to a furniture manufacturer on the grounds of a major fire loss sustained by the assured and a number of major losses sustained by others in the same business.

Add to the end of the paragraph:

17–64   **Over-valuation.** In *Strive Shipping Corp. v. Hellenic Mutual War Risks Association, The "Grecia Express"*, [2002] 2 All E.R. (Comm) 213, insurers sought to avoid for non-disclosure that a ferry valued at $8m only had a market value of about $4m to $5m. Colman J. held that they had to establish that the market value, if disclosed, would have influenced a prudent underwriter in as much as it suggested the risk of moral hazard. They failed to do this, as it was consistent with bona fide and prudent ship management to insure the ferry for much more than market value at the inception of the policy. In the event of the ferry's loss in mid season, a replacement of the same characteristics could reasonably be expected to cost $8m.

A different decision on materiality was reached in the misrepresentation case of *Eagle Star Insurance Co. v. Games Video Co* [2004] 1 All E.R. (Comm) 560, in which a vessel's value had been given as $1.8m whereas its true value was found to be only $100–$150,000. Here the assured was found to have deliberately presented false documents to insurers in order to support the higher value. The court accepted expert underwriting evidence that the excessively high value stated cast doubt upon the risk and the bona fides of the assured, following remarks made by Blackburn J. in *Ionides v. Pender* (1874) L.R. 9 Q.B. 531, at 538.

(e) *What Need not be Disclosed by the Assured*

Delete existing text and replace as follows:

17–73   **Constructive knowledge of insurers.** Section 18(3) of the Marine Insurance Act 1906 provides:

> "In the absence of inquiry the following circumstances need not be disclosed, namely:
>
> (a) ....
> (b) Any circumstance which is known or presumed to be known to the insurer.

The insurer is presumed to know matters of common notoriety or knowledge, and matters which an insurer in the ordinary course of his business, as such, ought to know; . . . .".

Sub-section 3(b) may also be taken to state the law applicable to non-marine insurances—*Pan Atlantic Ins. Co v. Pine Top Ins. Co* [1995] A.C. 501, 518, 554. The first sentence states the general principle that the assured need not disclose what the actual insurer either actually knows or is presumed to know. The second sentence defines those matters which the actual insurer is deemed to know. These are split into two categories. The first one includes matters of common knowledge and public awareness which any reasonably well-informed person is presumed to know from the media, for example, that forest fires occur in California. The second category covers matters which only an insurer ought to be aware of in his capacity as an insurer transacting a particular class of insurance business—for examples see paragraphs 17–74 to 17–77 below. So far as the Act itself is concerned, that is marine insurance business of one type or another. Once the sub-section is applied by analogy to non-marine insurance, such as film finance insurance, the second category covers matters which any insurer in the business of writing such risks ought to know, *qua* insurer and not as a well-informed member of the public, for example, that a preliminary estimate has been circulated in the market of the overall size of a number of recent film producers indemnity losses. It would not include the fact that a particular Hollywood film studio had intimated a claim because that is not general market intelligence disseminated to all insurers accepting film finance risks. Thus in *North British Fishing Boat Insurance v. Starr* (1922) 13 Ll. L. Rep. 206, 210, Rowlatt J. held that the increased general incidence of losses to British coastal fishing vessels was something which a reinsurer reinsuring this class of marine risk was presumed to know because it was his business to know it, but he would not be expected to know circumstances specially affecting particular ships or shipping lines. It follows that a marine insurer is not presumed to know about an item of general market intelligence concerning a particular ship or cargo, unless he was interested in it at the time that the report was circulated—*London General Insurance v. London Marine Underwriters' Association* [1921] 1 K.B. 104.

It has been held that presumed knowledge is not exhaustively defined by reference to what *an* insurer should know, but also by reference to what *the* actual insurer knows or should reasonably know from facts already in his possession—*Glencore International AG v. Alpina Ins. Co Ltd* [2004] 1 All E.R. (Comm) 766 [55], although the true construction of the sub-section was not there in issue. Information gained in the usual course of the actual insurer's business would include the state of his own reinsurances—*SAIL v. Farex Gie* [1995] 2 Lloyd's Rep.116, 156—and the existence of an excess of loss programme which the actual underwriter had previously had occasion to consider—*Kingscroft Ins. Co v. Nissan Fire & Marine Ins. Co* [1999]

Lloyd's Rep. I.R. 603,629–631 *obiter*. Presumed awareness has been held to extend to facts about which an insurer has the means of learning, from sources readily available to him, such information being described as "within his knowledge"—*Foley v. Tabor* (1862) 2 F. & F. 663.

Add to the end of the paragraph:

17–76 **Business practice and custom.** In *Glencore International AG v. Alpina Insurance Co. Ltd* [2004] 1 All E.R. (Comm) 766 at [37–41], Moore-Bick J. reviewed the authorities and held that an underwriter will be presumed to have in mind only such matters as would be within the contemplation of one who is familiar with the trade in question. It followed that when he was asked to write an open cover insuring worldwide shipments by a commodity trader, the range of circumstances with which he was taken to be familiar was very wide. The assured would still have to disclose any circumstances peculiar to the assured's business of which someone with knowledge of the particular trade in general terms would not be aware.

Add to n.74
  Mann MacNeal and Steeves Ltd v. Capital and Counties Ins. Co. Ltd. [1921] 2 K.B. 300.

Add to the end of the second paragraph:

17–80 **Assured's opinion.** In *Glencore International AG v. Alpina Insurance Co. Ltd.* 2004] 1 All E.R. (Comm) 766 [122], Moore-Bick J. said that:

> "The duty of disclosure requires the insured to place all material information fairly before the underwriter, but the underwriter must also play his part by listening carefully to what is said to him and cannot hold the insured responsible if by failing to do so he does not grasp the full implications of what he has been told".

Add to n.85:

  Iron Trades Mutual Ins. Co. Ltd. v. Cia. De Seguros Imperio [1991] 1 Re. L.R. 213.

Add to n.91:

17–82 **Facts covered by or dispensed with by a warranty or condition.** *International Management Group v. Simmonds* [2004] Lloyd's Rep. I.R. 247 [126] where Cooke J. said: "It is trite law that there is no need to make disclosure of facts or circumstances covered by a warranty in the insurance".

Add to the end of the paragraph:

Facts as to which the insurer waives information. This paragraph in the 10th edition of this work was approved and applied by the majority of the Court of Appeal in *WISE Underwriting Agency v. Grupo Nacional Provincial SA* [2004] 2 All E.R. (Comm) 613. The third member of the Court, Rix L.J., did not disapprove it, but was concerned to stress that the assured's presentation and the insurer's reaction are not so much separate stages in an enquiry as to waiver, but rather two sides of the same coin. Obviously a presentation is not unfair merely because the assured has not disclosed all material facts, because then waiver would never arise. The question is whether the presentation fairly puts the underwriter on notice, taking into account what he already knows and is presumed to know, that there are other material circumstances which he may wish to ask about. The more unusual these are, the clearer their existence should be indicated. If sufficient warning is given, it is then unfair for the insurer to seek to avoid a ground on which he ought to have satisfied himself at the time. **17–83**

Add to n.98:
Stowers v. GA Bonus Plc [2003] Lloyd's Rep. I.R. 402, 409.

Add to n.9:

Incomplete answers. *Stowers v. GA Bonus Plc* [2003] Lloyd's Rep. I.R. 402, where the proposal form asked: "During the last 5 years, have you sustained any losses ... whether or not insured?" If "YES", please state for each ...". The assured simply answered "Yes", giving no details. It was held that the underwriter was entitled to read this as referring to a single loss of which he had been told by the assured's broker, and did not waive disclosure of other claims of which he had not been told. **17–85**

(g) *Miscellaneous*

Add to text in point 3, after n.24:

Affirmation. An insurer is not entitled to suspend performance of the insurance contract while he decides whether to avoid it, and if he announces that he is doing so, runs the risk of repudiating the contract—*Glencore International AG v. Alpina Ins. Co Ltd* [2004] 1 All E.R. (Comm) 766 [308]. **17–90**

Add to text in point 4, after n.25:

In *Spriggs v. Wessington Court School* [2005] Lloyd's Rep. I.R. 474 at 480, Stanley Burnton J. identified an inconsistency between the statement by Mance J. in the *ICCI* case at p.174, that the test to be applied is whether a reasonable person in the position of the assured would have regarded insurers as making an unequivocal choice, and the statement by David Steel J. in *Callaghan v. Thompson* [2000] Lloyd's Rep. I.R. 125 at 134 said that the assured himself must appreciate that the insurers have made a choice, and held *obiter* that the objective test from *ICCI* was to be preferred to the subjective test from *Callaghan*. With respect, it may be doubted whether David Steel J. was intending to formulate a subjective test of knowledge, as at this point, he was disposing of a challenge to the principles laid down by Mance J. in the *ICCI* case. Another issue which arose in *Spriggs* was whether an unequivocal statement by liability insurers of their informed choice to keep the policy on foot made not to the assured but to solicitors acting for third party claimants, was sufficient to found an affirmation. The court held that communication to the assured was required, save in the rare case where it had become impossible by reason of the deliberate decision of the assured to make itself uncontactable, which was not established on the facts before it.

Add to text in point 5, after n.26:

In *Spriggs v. Wessington Court School* [2005] Lloyd's Rep. I.R. 474, a solicitor acting for insurers wrote a letter to the solicitor acting for third party claimants invoking the Third Party (Rights against Insurers) Act 1930, and said:

> "We write to confirm that Royal & Sun Alliance are on risk for Wessington Court School. We do not at this stage have details of the dates for which Wessington ... were covered by [RSA's] insurance policy ..."

It was argued that the use of the words "on risk" constituted a communication of an election by Royal & Sun Alliance not to avoid the policy in question for non-disclosure. The court held that in the context of preceding correspondence, it meant no more than that a policy had been issued to the school and could not reasonably be construed as an acceptance of liability for the claims being made.

Add to text in point 6, after n.31:

The issue of an unequivocal notice of cancellation, pursuant to the contract of insurance, can amount to its affirmation if this is done at a time when the insurers know that they have a right to avoid the insurance for non-disclosure—*WISE Underwriting Agency v. Grupo Nacional Provincial SA* [2004] 1 All E.R. (Comm) 613, 639, 653, approving *Mint Security v. Blair*

[1982] 1 Lloyd's Rep. 188,198 (avoidance for breach of warranty under the law in force prior to the decision in *The "Good Luck"* — see paragraph 10–88 above) and *Iron Trades Mutual Insurance Co Ltd v Cia de Seguros Imperio* [1991] 1 Re. L.R. 213, 225. On the other hand, it has been held that the exercise of a contractual right to inspect the assured's records is not an affirmation of the contract because such clauses, like arbitration clauses, are autonomous and independent of the substantive and primary provisions of the contract of insurance—*Strive Shipping Corp. v. Hellenic Mutual War Risks Association, The "Grecia Express"*, [2002] 2 All E.R. (Comm) 213, 319. *Sed contra Pan Atlantic Ins. Co. v. Pine Top Ins. Co.* [1992] 1 Lloyd's Rep. 101, 107–108. The renewal of a warehouseman's policy after receipt of a loss adjuster's report, stating that the assured had been in the practice of releasing goods to a customer without production of a bill of lading, constituted an affirmation of the insurance, and prevented insurers from avoiding for non-disclosure of this practice at placement—*Frans Maas (UK) Ltd v. Sun Alliance & London Ins. Plc* [2004] Lloyd's Rep. 649.

Add the following new paragraphs:

Unconscionability. Three recent decisions have addressed the question of whether, in appropriate cases, an insurer is precluded from exercising his right of avoidance because to do so would represent a breach of the duty to act with the utmost good faith and would amount to unconscionable conduct. **17–90A**

In *Strive Shipping Corp. v Hellenic War Risks Association, The "Grecia Express"*, [2002] 2 All E.R. (Comm) 213, the court was concerned with non-disclosure of alleged criminality and misconduct by the alter ego of the assured company, one V, and that prior losses had occurred in suspicious circumstances, which would cause a prudent underwriter to have doubts about the magnitude of the proposed risk and the moral integrity of V. Colman J. heard evidence about the circumstances in which the losses occurred. He found that there had been no criminality or misconduct on V's part and that the suspicions attaching to them were unjustified, so that there had been no material facts to be disclosed. He added that if there had been an actual allegation made prior to placement that V had wilfully brought about one loss, it should have been disclosed although he had held that it would have been unfounded. However, he went on to hold that the court would have held that insurers' avoidance of the insurance for non-disclosure of that allegation was impermissible because it would have been unfounded, so that they would have been in breach of their duty of good faith. Similarly, if contrary to his own opinion, the suspicions attaching to the losses should have been disclosed, it would have been inconsistent with their duty to act in good faith for insurers to maintain their avoidance of the insurance after it was established that the suspicions were unfounded. The learned judge's reasons were that the court's jurisdiction to avoid an insurance contract for non-disclosure was derived from the equitable jurisdiction to rescind for misrepresentation. Accordingly, the court could not sanction the insurers' avoidance of the contract in circumstances where it would be unconscionable, and that it was unconscionable, because contrary to the duty of utmost good faith, for an insurer to avoid an insurance for non-disclosure of allegations and suspicions which had been found to be baseless after the insurer had elected to avoid it—[2002] 2 All E.R. (Comm) 213, 270, 275, 306.

17–90B In *Brotherton v. Aseguradora Colseguros SA* [2003] 2 All E.R. (Comm) 298, the court was concerned with non-disclosure by a re-assured to reinsurers, of reports in the Columbian press that allegations had been made of misconduct on the part of the original assured bank's president and others, and that an investigation into it was being pursued by the Procurador General of Columbia. The reinsured admitted the reports but contended that their materiality and the reinsurers' entitlement to avoid depended upon whether the allegations were correct so that there was actual misconduct, and that there should be a trial of that issue. The issue arose on the reinsurers' application to strike out the paragraphs of the reinsured's pleading, which denied that there was a proper basis for an investigation and alleged that the allegations made against those individuals were baseless. Reliance was placed on the *"Grecia Express"* case.

The Court of Appeal disapproved the reasoning of Colman J. summarised above. Firstly, the materiality of the undisclosed reports depended upon circumstances known at the time of placement and not on a subsequent enquiry into their validity. It was unsound to introduce into English law a principle that an assured could resist avoidance for non-disclosure of an allegation or intelligence by insisting on a trial of its truth which could be costly, difficult, and oppressive to insurers. Secondly, it was incorrect that the reinsurers' right to avoid was conditional upon avoidance being consistent with good faith or conscience. Even assuming that avoidance was an equitable remedy, which was open to doubt and had been left open in the case of *Pan Atlantic Ins. Co. v. Pine Top Ins. Co.* [1995] 1 A.C. 501, at page 544, it was not a sufficient reason to make it conditional upon the utmost good faith of the insurer exercising it. In any case, it was hard to see how an insurer was acting contrary to good faith if, when he elected to avoid the insurance, he did not know for a fact that the allegation or intelligence was baseless. Thirdly, again assuming avoidance to be similar to rescission, it took effect upon the act of the insurer communicating his election to avoid, and independently of the court—*Drake Insurance Plc v. Provident insurance Plc* [2003] 1 All E.R. (Comm) 759. The role of the court was to rule whether or not the declaration of avoidance was valid, and avoidance did not depend upon the court decreeing that the insurance contract was avoided. Accordingly, the Court upheld the decision of Moore-Bick J. to strike out the relevant paragraphs of the reinsured's pleadings—[2003] 1 All E.R. (Comm) 774.

The question of whether the insurer's duty to act in the utmost good faith **17–90C** could fetter his exercise of the right to avoid for misrepresentation or non-disclosure, was considered again by a differently constituted Court of Appeal in *Drake Insurance Plc v. Provident Insurance Plc* [2004] Q.B. 601. The facts were very different from those in the previous case of *Brotherton*, and are described in paragraph 17–56 above. A motor insurer sought to avoid a motor policy for non-disclosure of a speeding conviction which, if taken with a previous accident provisionally classified as caused by the fault of the assured, entitled the insurer to demand a higher premium. The assured also failed to advise the insurer that the third party involved in the accident had accepted responsibility and had paid for the damage to the insured vehicle. The insurer was not told about this until after it had avoided the insurance. Had this been known to the insurer at placement, it would have counter-balanced the speeding conviction and the premium would have remained the same. The insurer had therefore avoided the policy in ignorance of circumstances at the time of placement, which rendered the un-disclosed speeding conviction immaterial under the rating system which it applied. Moreover, the Court held that this would have come to light at placement if disclosure of the latter had been made. It was argued that the failure of the motor insurer to enquire whether the "fault" accident had been settled and reclassified as "no fault" was inconsistent with its duty to act in good faith, and so disentitled it to avoid when it did.

The majority of the Court (Rix and Clarke L.JJ.), allowed the appeal on other grounds and refrained from deciding this point. However, they did express *obiter* opinions on it. Rix L.J. said that it was not open to the Court to go behind the trial judge's finding that the motor insurer had acted in complete good faith when it decided to avoid the policy. This was fatal to the submission, he said. While expressing some sympathy with the idea that good faith required an insurer to give the assured an opportunity to address the reason for an intended avoidance, he noted that this was not yet the law [92]. Clarke L.J. agreed [145]. However, Pill L.J. held that good faith obliged the insurer to check the status of the accident before exercising the draco-nian and "wholly one-sided" remedy of avoidance [177].

The present state of the law appears to be that an assured cannot defeat avoidance on the ground that it is unconscionable. However, we have submitted in paragraph 17–2 of the 10th edition of this work that the over-riding principle of good faith may serve as a basis for the implication of implied terms, to qualify the exercise of remedies by the insurer in order to prevent unfairness to the assured. It is, we submit, not too far fetched to suggest that by an implied term of a policy of insurance, an insurer agrees to give notice to the assured of the grounds of an intended avoidance of the policy.

Additional evidence of breach by assured. In *Spriggs v. Wessington Court* **17–90D** *School* [2005] Lloyd's Rep. I.R. 474, the issue arose whether after an insurer has affirmed the contract of insurance, the subsequent discovery of additional undisclosed facts will give rise to a fresh right to avoid the insurance. The court held *obiter* that, if the new material would make a material difference to the reasonable insurer's decision whether or not to affirm, it would recreate a new right to avoid for non-disclosure. It may be that the words "would make" should be read as "would have made". It is submitted that the result must be correct if the new facts are separate from the previously discovered facts. There have then been separate breaches of the assured's duty of disclosure. The position is not so clear when the new facts are merely additional examples of the same sort of circumstances, in respect of which the insurer elected to affirm the insurance contract. In *Spriggs* the court held that, if the insurers had affirmed after discovering the pre-placement non-disclosure of four complaints from former pupils of sexual abuse by staff at the insured school, the subsequent discovery that a further 23 former pupils had also made complaints, would have re-created a right to avoid the liability policies in question. It could be said that the insurers had waived their right to avoid the policies for failure to disclose the existence of this kind of circumstance, likely to give rise to claims. Alternatively, it might be thought unjust to insurers who decided to continue the cover in the knowledge that they had a defence only to a few claims, only to be unable to avoid it when there turned out to be a defence to over five times as many for which the assured's potential liability was far greater. The court's holding supports the latter view. No doubt it is a matter of degree in each case.

Delete existing text and replace as follows:

17–91 **Exclusion of duty and of remedy for breach.** The law will enforce a clause in a contract of insurance, which unequivocally releases the assured from his duty of disclosure—*Svebska Handelsbank v. Sun Alliance & London Ins. Plc* [1966] 1 Lloyd's Rep. 519, 551; *Sumitomo Bank Ltd. v. Banque Bruxelles Lambert SA* [1997] 1 Lloyd's Rep. 487, 495; *HIH Casualty & General Ins. Ltd v. Chase Manhattan Bank* [2003] 1 All E.R. (Comm) 349—or which restricts or excludes the exercise by the insurer of his right to avoid the contract in the event of the assured's breach of the duty of disclosure—*Arab Bank Ltd v. Zurich Ins. Co.* [1999] 1 Lloyd's Rep. 262; *Kumar v. AGF Ins. Ltd* [1998] 4 All E.R. 788; *Pan Atlantic Ins. Co v. Pine Top Ins. Co* [1993] 1 Lloyd's Rep. 496, 502; *HIH Casualty & General Ins. Ltd v. Chase Manhattan Bank* [2003] 1 All E.R. (Comm) 349. Neither the duty of utmost good faith nor any other rule of public policy invalidates such provisions, with the exception of fraudulent concealment by the assured—*HIH Casualty & General Ins. Ltd v. Chase Manhattan Bank, supra.* Where the assured is released from his duty of disclosure, it does not follow without more that the assured's agent to insure is released from his own duty of disclosure—*HIH Casualty & General Ins. Ltd v. Chase Manhattan Bank, supra,* reversing

[2001] 2 Lloyd's Rep. 483, 507–509 and distinguishing *SAIL v. Farex Gie* [1995] L.R.L.R. 116, 157. Where the right to avoid is excluded, it is still an open question of whether the law countenances a clause which clearly extends the waiver to dishonest non-disclosure on the part of the agent to insure—*HIH Casualty & General Ins. Ltd v. Chase Manhattan Bank, supra,* where the clause in question was insufficiently worded to demonstrate such an intention.

CHAPTER 19

THE LOSS

1. Causation

Add at the end of the paragraph:

Two effective causes. In *Tektrol Ltd v. International Insurance Co of* **19–5**
Hanover Ltd. [2005] 1 All E.R. (Comm) 132, the rule that the assured will
not recover when loss is caused by two causes and one is an excluded cause,
was extended to a case where one cause was an indirect and not proximate
cause of the loss, but was within an exclusion of loss "arising directly or
indirectly" from certain events. The assured owned a source code held in five
different locations. All five copies were lost as a result of two entirely
unrelated events, the first being an email virus which corrupted two locations, and the second being a burglary in which computers and a hard copy
of a print-out of the code were stolen, these being the remaining three
locations. A business interruption claim was submitted to insurers under an
all risks policy. It was common ground that the burglary had caused the
loss. The virus had created an increased risk of loss by eliminating two
copies of the code. Langley J. held that this was sufficient to give it a causal
relationship to the loss, because there would have been no loss if the virus
had not reduced the appropriate protection for the code. It was therefore an
indirect cause of the loss and not mere history [12]. He then applied the

principle from *Wayne Tank & Pump Co v. The Employers' Liability Assurance Corp. Ltd, supra,* noting that the two or more causes need not be exactly co-extensive in time—*Handelsbanken ASA v. Dandridge* [2002] 2 All E.R. (Comm) 39 at [47] *per* Potter L.J. The virus was an excluded cause of loss because the corruption or erasure of the source code was "caused deliberately" by the creators of the virus. "Deliberately" meant "done on purpose" and the insurers did not have to show that it was targeted at the assured in particular, rather than anyone else. The assured's claim failed. Since the learned judge went on to hold that loss caused by the burglary was also excluded, his extension of the *Wayne Tank* rule is probably strictly speaking *obiter.*

Another case in which *Wayne Tank* was applied is *Midland Mainline v. Eagle Star Insurance Co.* [2004] Lloyd's Rep. I.R., in which a train operating company had made a claim for business interruption losses caused by the imposition of emergency speed restrictions following the Hatfield train crash in October 2000. The speed restrictions were imposed in places where "gauge corner cracking" had been identified. This was a form of wear and tear, or "rolling contact fatigue". There was an exclusion of wear and tear. The Court of Appeal decided that this wear and tear was either the sole proximate cause of the assured's loss or at least a concurrent proximate cause alongside the imposition of the speed restrictions. Since the principle from *Wayne Tank* is that an express exclusion always takes priority over express words of coverage, this was enough to defeat the claim. The submission that the Hatfield crash was itself the sole proximate cause of the loss was rejected, even in relation to the section of line where the crash occurred.

3. AMOUNT OF LOSS PAYABLE

(a) *General rules*

Add to end of text, after n.46:

19–10   **Valued policy.** The use of the words "sum insured" without words of valuation is a statement of the insurer's maximum liability under the policy. These words serve to fix a figure by which the premium can be calculated and which constitutes the upper limit of recovery—*Thor Navigation Inc v. Ingosstrakh Insurance* [2005] Lloyd's Rep. I.R. 490 [18].

Add to end of text after n.68:

19–16   **Value of property after loss.** A similar approach was followed in *Quorum A/S v. Schramm* [2002] 1 Lloyd's Rep. 249, where the damaged property consisted of a work of art, *La Danse Grecque*, by Degas, which sustained physical damage in a fire. The picture had to be valued for the purpose of a claim on a fine art policy. This was not a valued policy. Thomas J. took as the measure of the indemnity to which the assured was entitled the difference between the value of the picture before the fire and its value after restoration following the fire, but assessed hypothetically as if this had been completed immediately after the fire. The market value of the picture before the fire was based upon the price obtainable between a willing seller and a willing buyer in the private dealers' market rather than at auction, the former being likely to yield a higher price. It followed that no account was taken of the actual price realised for the restored picture about four years after the fire.

4. NOTICE OF LOSS

Add to n.19:

Condition precedent. *Pilkington United Kingdom Ltd v. CGU Insurance plc* **19–35**
[2005] 1 All E.R. (Comm) 283, 301.

Add to the end of the paragraph:

To whom notice must be given. In *Friends Provident Life and Pensions Ltd* **19–42**
v. Sirius International Insurance Corp. [2004] 2 All E.R. (Comm) 707, the question arose whether the assured under a professional indemnity cover with a primary layer and an excess layer could fulfil his duty to give notice to the insurers on the excess layer of a circumstance which might give rise to a claim by giving notice of it to those on the primary layer. The primary layer policy obliged the assured to notify the underwriters of such a circumstance "as soon as possible during the period of this policy". Any claim arising therefrom was deemed to be made in that same policy period, a provision of great importance in liability policies. This clause was held to be incorporated into the excess layer policy by general words of incorporation, and in that context the words "the underwriters" referred to the primary layer insurers, while the words "this policy" referred to the excess policy, so that the excess policy would also respond to a claim made outside the policy period if it arose from the notified circumstance, so long as notice was given in the period of the policy. It followed that timely notice to the primary layer insurers of a circumstance which might give rise to a claim, served to bring any claim arising therefrom within the excess layer, whether made within or without the period of the excess layer policy. The court's construction of the excess policy was consistent with the presumption that the scope of cover provided by an excess layer is intended to be identical to that provided by

the underlying layer. The decision on this part of the case was upheld on appeal—[2005] 2 All E.R. (Comm) 145.

Add new paragraph as follows:

19–46A   Sometimes a policy contains a condition that no claim is payable unless, if it has been made and rejected, action or suit has been brought within a stipulated time limit after the rejection. In *Super Chem Products Ltd v. American Life and General Ins. Co. Ltd* [2004] 1 All E.R. (Comm) 713, the fire policy covering the assured company's stock provided:

> "Condition 19: In no case whatever shall the Company be liable for any loss or damage after the expiration of twelve months from the happening of the loss or damage unless the claim is the subject of pending action or arbitration".

An action for payment of a loss was brought out of time. The assured established that negotiations with the insurer continued past the time at which the time bar expired, and contended that the insurer had thereby waived its right to rely on the limitation provision. The Privy Council held that the assured had failed to show that the insurers made an unequivocal representation that they would not rely on the time bar. The mere act of continuing negotiations was equivocal, and did not give rise to an estoppel, particularly as the insurer did not know whether or not a protective writ had been issued before the time bar expired.

The same question arose in *Fortisbank SA v. Trenwick International Ltd* [2005] Lloyd's Rep. I.R. 464, where a "fraudulent receivables" policy contained a condition requiring any legal proceedings for the recovery of a loss to be brought within 24 months from the time at which the loss was discovered. The assured began proceedings 17 months after the 24 months limitation period had expired, and contended that insurers had impliedly agreed not to rely on the time bar, but alternatively had waived their right to rely on it by requesting particulars of loss after it had expired. Gloster J. held that proof of the implied agreement required the assured to show that there had been an offer by insurers not to rely on the limitation clause, followed by acceptance and valuable consideration on the part of the assured, and this was lacking. The plea of waiver amounted to a defence of promissory estoppel. The Court stated the following legal principles applicable in relation to limitation clauses:

1. The insurers must be shown to have made a clear, unequivocal, unambiguous and unconditional promise to forgo a time bar defence—*Seechurn v. Ace* [2002] 2 Lloyd's Rep. 390, [26].
2. The promise relied upon must be construed objectively and be reasonably understood to be one to forgo that defence—*ibid*. It

follows that if the assured is unaware of the insurers' entitlement to rely on a time bar at the time in question, the defence will probably fail—*HIH Casualty & General Insurance Ltd v. Axa Corporate Solutions* [2003] Lloyd's Rep. I.R. 1 [22].

3. The mere fact that the insurers are prepared to negotiate with the assured about the claim, both before and after the expiration of the time bar, does not per se amount to a waiver or estoppel, because it does not show an unequivocal promise not to take a time bar defence if negotiations fail.

4. The assured must also establish that it attached significance to the insurers' unequivocal promise and in reliance on it altered its position to its detriment or in such other manner that it would be inequitable for insurers not to be held to their promise—*Seechurn v. Ace, supra; HIH Casualty & General Insurance Ltd v. Axa Corporate Solutions* [2003] Lloyd's Rep. I.R. 1 [29].

5. Once the limitation period has expired, it is in reality impossible for the assured to alter its position to its detriment in reliance upon any promise not to take a limitation defence, because the claim was already time-expired—*Seechurn v. Ace supra, [59]*.

Applying these principles, Gloster J. held that no estoppel was established. The mere fact that the insurers were engaged in investigating the assured's claim before and after the time bar expired was insufficient both for promissory estoppel and estoppel by convention.

5. Particulars and Proof of Loss

Add to n.75:

Particulars required. *Challenge Finance Ltd v. State Insurance General Manager* [1982] 1 N.Z.L.R. 762, 766–767; *Super Chem Products Ltd v. American Life and General Ins. Co Ltd* [2004] 1 All E.R. (Comm.) 713, 725.   **19–48**

6. Fraudulent Claims

Add to n.7:

Introductory. The supposed rule that after an insurer had alleged fraud against his assured he could not rely on clauses in the policy affording a defence to a claim, said to be based upon *Jureidini v. National British & Irish Millers Ins. Co Ltd* [1915] A.C. 499, was held by the Privy Council in the *Super Chem* case *supra* to be unsound. An insurer was entitled to defend a   **19–54**

claim on alternative bases, one of which may be fraud. *Jureidini* was no longer an authoritative decision in insurance law—[2004] 1 All E.R. (Comm) 713, [11–20].

(b) *The Common Law Rule*

Add to the end of the paragraph:

19–60   **Ambit of the rule.** In *Eagle Star Insurance Co. v. Games Video Co.* [2004] 1 All E.R. (Comm) 560, Simon J. found that the assured had deliberately supplied false and deceitful documents to insurers in order to support their claim for the constructive total loss of their vessel. The insurers argued that the claim must fail because fraudulent devices had been used to promote the claim by supporting an exaggerated value. Simon J. noted that the rule was anomalous in that it applied only between the making of the claim and the start of litigation, and that thereafter the assured might advance false documents and lie without the drastic consequences which follow if the deployment of the false documents and lies was, as he described it, "less well-timed" [150]. Nevertheless, he held that the rule was well-established and followed the definition given by Mance L.J. in the *Agapitos* case at [30]:

> "A fraudulent device is used if the insured believes he has suffered the loss claimed, but seeks to improve or embellish the facts surrounding the claim by some lie".

He added that the consequence was that the claim would be defeated, making no mention of forfeiture of the benefit of the policy. On the facts before him the distinction was not material.

Add to n.47:

19–61   In *Direct Line Insurance v. Khan* [2002] Lloyd's Rep. I.R. 364, the Court of Appeal again left open the question of whether the forfeit of all benefit involved the retrospective avoidance of the contract of insurance, as opposed to the loss of the fraudulent claim, as the insurers were only claiming repayment of the monies the subject of the fraudulent claim, and not of earlier claims [28]. A submission by the assureds that the common law rule was penal and unfair, and therefore invalidated by The Unfair Terms in Consumer Contracts Regulations 1994, was rejected because the Regulations did not apply to rules of law as opposed to the express terms of a consumer contract.

Add to the end of the paragraph:

Forfeiture of benefit. When the insurers in *Interpart Commerciao e Gestao*   **19–61**
SA v. Lexington Insurance Co [2004] Lloyd's Rep. I.R. 690 applied for
summary judgment against their assured on the ground that fraudulent
devices had been used to promote a claim, H.H. Judge Chambers Q.C.
refused it, partly for the reason that the law was in such a state of development as to merit a trial [44]. In *Marc Rich Agriculture Trading SA v.*
Fortis Corporate Insurance NV [2005] Lloyd's Rep. I.R. 396, Cooke J. was
faced with the reverse situation in which the assured sought summary
dismissal of the insurer's defence which alleged that fraudulent concealment
of material facts by the assured while prosecuting a claim amounted to the
use of a "fraudulent device". The assured argued that the court should
follow the "tentative view" of Mance L.J. in *Agapitos v. Agnew* [2003] Q.B.
556 [45] that dishonest concealment of matters which might prejudice the
insurers' consideration of the claim was not caught by the common law rule,
which required a lie or dishonest misrepresentation. Cooke J. noted that
what Mance L.J. had said was both tentative and *obiter*, and concluded that
this was undoubtedly a difficult, contentious and developing area of the law
[28]. The court's approach would differ depending on whether one applied
the common law rule requiring a clear lie or misrepresentation or section 17
of the 1906 Act, requiring the assured not to conceal material facts in bad
faith. At this stage it could not be said that Mance L.J. was so clearly right
as to merit striking out the insurers' defence.

There seem to be two questions which Cooke J. considered to be unresolved. The first is whether dishonest concealment by the assured when
presenting a claim can constitute a fraudulent device within the scope of the
common law rule. The second is whether it provides the insurer with a
defence under section 17. In paragraph 19–63 of the 10th edition of this
work, we have taken the view that it does not. However, the learned authors
of *Good Faith and Insurance Contracts*, suggest the opposite when they say
that the defence could attract the sanction of avoidance under section 17
(2nd ed. 2004), paragraph 11.42 *et seq.*, so that the insurers could rely on the
section independently of the common law rule.

More recently, the uncertainty of the law in this area has been diminished
by the decision of the Court of Appeal in *Axa General Insurance Ltd v.*
Gottlieb [2005] 1 All E.R. (Comm) 445. In this case the insured householders
made four claims under their buildings policy and payments were made by
insurers. False documents were prepared and used in furtherance of two of
the claims. On discovery of the fraud, insurers claimed repayment of all
monies paid by them in response to all four claims, relying on the common
law rule in relation to fraudulent claims. It was held that the common law
rule did not cause the assured to forfeit sums paid in settlement of other
claims made honestly, and before any fraud was perpetrated. In other
words, it did not have a retrospective effect on prior separate claims already

settled under the same policy before any fraud occurred. The hypothetical question of whether the fraud would bar payment of a prior honest claim awaiting settlement was left open, although the logic of the decision suggests that it would not do so. The assureds sought to retain interim payments made by insurers in settlement of one of the fraudulent claims, prior to the time at which false documents were used to obtain payment of a final balance. The Court held that the entire claim was forfeit, and it made no difference whether sums were outstanding or had been actually advanced in partial payment before a fraud was committed by the assured. Such sums had been paid in satisfaction of a cause of action which was retrospectively undone or barred by the fraud.

The decision in *Gottlieb* is to be welcomed for the clarification it affords of the working of the common law rule. Unfortunately, the availability to an insurer of different remedies in response to a fraudulent claim means that this area of the law continues to be far from simple.

7. INTEREST & COSTS

Delete the second paragraph and footnotes 70 and 71 and replace as follows:

19–67   **Interest runs from date of default.** The court may abridge the period for the running of interest or reduce the rate of interest to mark its disapproval of the claimant's delay in bringing or pursuing his claim, although this has the effect of providing a windfall to the insurer who should not have had the use of the money—*Whiting v. New Zealand Ins. Co* (1932) 44 Ll.L.Rep.179, 181; *Metal Box Ltd v. Currys* [1988] 1 All E.R. 341, 346; *Adcock v. Co-Operative Ins. Soc. Ltd* [2000] Lloyd's Rep. I.R. 657, 663–664; *Kuwait Airways Corp. v. Kuwait Ins. Co* [2000] Lloyd's Rep. I.R. 678,689; *Quorum A/S v. Schramm (No 2)* [2002] 2 All E.R. (Comm) 179; *Hellenic Industrial Development Bank v. Atkin* [2003] Lloyd's Rep. I.R. 365. It can be explained on the basis that the assured's unreasonable delay becomes a cause of the money remaining unpaid—*Kuwait Airways Corp. v. Kuwait Ins. Co, supra; Quorum A/S v. Schramm (No 2), supra* at page 186.

Add to n.79:

19–70   **Compensation for unreasonable delay in payment.** An unsuccessful attempt to circumvent this rule was made in *Normhurst Ltd v. Dornoch Ltd.* [2005] Lloyd's Rep. I.R. 27, in which it was argued that the insurer's primary liability under a combined commercial property and business interruption policy was not to pay damages, but to make a "contractual payment". The court held that the policy was indisputably an indemnity policy to which the rule applied.

CHAPTER 20

THE CLAIMANT

1. ASSIGNMENT

(a) *Voluntary assignment*

Add to the end of the paragraph:

Assignment of policy contrasted with assignment of right of recovery. In   **20–5**
Bestquest Ltd v. Regency Care Group Ltd [2003] Lloyd's Rep. I.R. 392, the
court was concerned with the failure of a vendor of a building, together with
the business carried on therein, to cause the purchaser's interest to be noted
on the vendor's insurance covering both damage to the building and loss of
income through business interruption caused thereby. The contract of sale
required this to be done in order to protect the purchaser against the
occurrence of such loss between the date of exchange of contracts and the
date for completion. A flood during this period caused damage to the
building and consequential business interruption, but the vendor had not
caused the purchaser's interest to be noted on the policy before it occurred.
After completion, the insurers paid the vendors for the physical damage to
the buildings and the money was paid over to the purchaser, but neither the
vendor nor the purchaser could bring a claim on the policy for loss caused
by business interruption, since the vendor had suffered no loss and the
purchaser had no right of suit on the policy. The purchaser raised a claim
for substantial damages for loss caused to it by this breach of duty. In a

71

hearing dealing with preliminary issues, the purchaser argued that, if its interest had been noted on the policy, that would have constituted notice to the insurers of the assignment to it of all the vendor's rights under the policy, so that it could have recovered for its loss of income from business interruption, citing *Colonial Mutual General Ins. Co v. ANZ Banking Group Ltd* [1995] 1 W.L.R. 1140. The court distinguished *Colonial Mutual* on the ground that the mortgagee was entitled to recover the proceeds of insurance payable to the mortgagor, and that the notice of the former's interest perfected an equitable assignment of the policy monies. However, in *Bestquest* the purchaser would have been making a claim which the vendor of the business could not have made. It dismissed, however, the vendor's submission that the insurers could and would have refused to consent to the assignment. It is submitted with respect that, as the learned judge implicitly held, the contract of sale contained an assignment of the vendor's policy and not merely of the proceeds of a claim, so that the consent of the insurers was required and had not been obtained. This part of his decision must rest on the inference drawn from the insurers' pleading that they would not have refused consent and must be treated as *obiter*, seeing that the policy was not in evidence, and that this was not one of the preliminary issues stated for decision.

Add to n.34:

20–7   **Consent of the insurer.** For the normal practice of life insurers in requiring proof of the assignment of a life policy, see *N M Rothschild & Sons (CI) Ltd v. Equitable Life Assurance Society* [2003] Lloyd's Rep. I.R. 371.

2. LIMITED INTERESTS IN PROPERTY

(b) *Bailor and Bailee*

Delete the text between nn.1 and 2 and replace as follows:

20–24   **Insurance by bailee.** He may, of course, insure only his own liability in respect of goods entrusted to him, by taking out an insurance "on goods held in trust and for which he is responsible", in which case he will recover an indemnity in the event of a loss only against the amount of his liability (if any) to their owner and not necessarily their full value—see paragraph 1–182 *ante*, but he often insures for the full value either because he has agreed with the goods-owner to do so, or because he knows that full value insurance will operate as an inducement to potential bailors to place their goods in his hands[2].

Add to n.1:

For a recent case confirming that a bailee's insurance may cover only his own liability, see *Ramco (U.K.) Ltd v. International Ins. Co. of Hannover Ltd* [2004] Lloyd's Rep. I.R. 606; see para.1–182, *ante*.

3. CLAIMS BROUGHT BY THIRD PARTIES PURSUANT TO THE CONTRACTS (RIGHTS OF THIRD PARTIES) ACT 1999

Insert in text after n.52

Reinsurance agreements in some foreign jurisdictions sometimes contain **20–66** so called "cut-through" clauses, affording the original assured a direct right of action against the reinsurer in the event of the reinsured's insolvency. The 1999 Act has removed one obstacle to such clauses in the form of the doctrine of privity, but another obstacle remains in the form of the central insolvency principle that unsecured creditors must be treated equally. The effect of a cut-through clause is to give the assured a prior claim on the most valuable asset of an insolvent insurer, his potential reinsurance recoveries. In *Grecoair Inc v. Tilling* [2005] Lloyd's Rep. I.R. 151, an aeroplane was insured against hull and liability risks by the Angolan insurer ENSA, which was in turn reinsured by Lloyd's syndicates, and a claims control clause in the reinsurance delegated claims handling to the reinsurers. The aircraft was damaged by a fork lift truck and a motor truck respectively in two separate accidents and two claims were made. The underlying policy contained a "cut-through clause" concerning two other insured aircraft, but in reality this was a form of loss payee clause in favour of a finance house. The assured submitted that the two contracts gave it a direct right of recourse against Lloyd's syndicates. This argument predictably failed on the true construction of the insurance documents. The assured then argued that there had been an oral agreement that the reinsurers would assume a direct liability towards it, but the court was unable to find that any such offer capable of acceptance had been made.

Add to n.52:

This difficulty would not be present if C was B's registered civil partner because under the Civil Partnerships Act 2004, s.253, the presumption that one spouse has an unlimited insurable interest in the life of the other is extended to civil partners.

CHAPTER 22

SUBROGATION

2. Conditions Precedent to the Exercise of Rights of Subrogation

(c) *Exclusion of Rights of Subrogation*

Add to n.14:

See also *BP Exploration Operating Co. Ltd v. Kvaerner Oilfield Products**22–33**
Ltd* [2005] 1 Lloyd's Rep. 307, where, in a construction all risks policy, it
was accepted that a waiver of subrogation would be co-extensive with the
cover to be effected by the principal assured for the benefit of a co-assured
under the terms of the contract between them.

3. Exercise of Rights of Subrogation

(a) *Claims against Third Parties*

Add to the end of the paragraph as follows:

In *T & N Ltd v. Royal & Sun Alliance plc (No. 2)* [2004] Lloyd's Rep. I.R. **22–38**
106, the assured had employer's liability insurance with Lloyd's

underwriters, under the terms of which it was obliged to reimburse the underwriters against claims and expenses up to a certain amount. It effected insurance against that liability with another insurer, C. It was held that the underwriters could have no rights of subrogation against C. Such a right was only exercisable in respect of the loss against which the assured was insured, namely their liability to their employees.

4. COMMENCEMENT AND CONDUCT OF PROCEEDINGS

Add text after n.48 as follows:

22–43   **Insurer has no right to sue in own name.** So, the insurers are subject to the action being time-barred under the Limitation Act 1980 in the same way as the assured: *Graham v. Entec Europe Ltd* [2004] Lloyd's Rep. I.R. 660, where the insurers were deemed to have the knowledge of the loss adjuster they appointed for the purposes of section 14A of the Limitation Act 1980. The words "the plaintiff" in section 14A(5) (the limitation period starts to run "from the earliest date upon which the plaintiff ... first had both the knowledge required for bringing an action ... and a right to bring such an action") included an insurer suing by way of subrogation.

7. APPLICATION TO PARTICULAR CASES

Add to n.78:

22–98   **The insurance policy—express waiver.** *BP Exploration Operating Co. Ltd v. Kvaerner Oilfield Products Ltd* [2005] 1 Lloyd's Rep. 307.

Add to n.87:

22–100   **The implied term analysis.** *BP Exploration Operating Co. Ltd v. Kvaerner Oilfield Products Ltd* [2005] 1 Lloyd's Rep. 307—if a party is not identified as a co-assured in the policy, the assured must have assumed a contractual obligation to him to procure the benefit of cover for him; a mere intention to do so is not sufficient.

CHAPTER 23

RIGHTS OF TWO OR MORE INSURERS

1. DOUBLE INSURANCE

The same interest. These paragraphs were cited with approval in *O'Kane v.* **23–8**
Jones [2005] Lloyd's Rep. I.R. 174, 209, 210. **and**
23–9

Add to the end of the paragraph as follows:
The decision in *Nichols & Co. v. Scottish Union and National Insurance* **23–15**
Co. was regarded as of questionable value in *O'Kane v. Jones* [2005] Lloyd's
Rep. I.R. 174, 211.

Add at the end of the paragraph as follows:

Rateable proportion of loss. In *Drake Insurance plc v. Provident Insurance* **23–20**
plc [2004] Q.B. 601, at paragraph 120, Rix L.J. commented, in the context of
the situation where one insurer is arguing that it is not contractually liable,
that it was:

> "a matter of concern that an insurer who takes a premium to cover 100
> per cent of a risk may only be liable for 50 per cent of a loss on the basis
> that the insured can obtain the other half elsewhere."

See also the discussion of this decision at paragraph 23–27, *post*. In *Phillips
v. Syndicate 992 Gunner* [2004] Lloyd's Rep. I.R. 426, Eady J. easily rejected

an argument that a rateable proportion clause in an employer's liability policy could be in any way applicable to successive policies of insurance.

Add to the end of the paragraph as follows:

23–27   However, in *O'Kane v. Jones* [2005] Lloyd's Rep. I.R. 174, Richard Siberry Q.C., sitting as a Deputy High Court Judge, preferred the reasoning in *Legal and General Assurance v. Drake Insurance* to that in *Eagle Star Insurance v. Provincial Insurance* and regarded himself as bound, as a judge of first instance, to follow the Court of Appeal decision rather than the advice of the Privy Council. However, the facts here were very different. The insurer denying its liability to contribute had agreed with the assured to cancel the policy after the loss. In such circumstances it does seem equitable that he should nonetheless be regarded as liable to make a contribution.

In different and complex circumstances, the Court of Appeal in *Drake Insurance plc v. Provident Insurance plc* [2004] Q.B. 601 doubted aspects of the decision in *Legal and General Assurance v. Drake Insurance*. Here K was liable for a motor accident when driving her husband's car with his consent. She was insured under her own policy with Drake when driving any car with the owner's consent. She was also a named driver under her husband's policy with Provident. Provident purported to avoid its policy for non-disclosure and initially that was upheld in arbitration and at the first instance, although the Court of Appeal reversed that decision (see paragraph 17–28, 17–56 and 17–90C *ante*). In these circumstances Drake indemnified her fully against her liability, despite the presence of a rateable proportion clause in its policy, and then claimed a contribution from Provident. The Court of Appeal held that it was entitled to a contribution, rejecting the argument from Provident that, in paying the full amount of the claim, Drake had acted as a volunteer. Ultimately, this was based on the fact that Drake had paid the full amount only because at the time Provident had successfully avoided its policy and therefore Drake had protested its right to a contribution. Thus Drake could not possibly be said to be a volunteer.

However, views expressed by the judges cast some doubt on the extent to which they would have allowed a rateable proportion clause to exclude or limit the right of contribution, in particular expressing their doubts as to the reasoning of Ralph Gibson L.J. in *Legal and General Insurance v. Drake Insurance* (see paragraph 23–26) and proffering what might be regarded as a slightly different interpretation of the Privy Council's advice to that indicated earlier in this paragraph. Rix L.J. commented (at paragraph 114):

> "...it seems to me that Ralph Gibson L.J. was ... going further than the logic of the decision of this court in *Legal and General v Drake* required, as was demonstrated by the Privy Council's decision and reasoning in *Eagle Star*. ...[T]he Privy Council did not regard the mere existence of the rateable proportion clause as excluding the operation of

the equitable right to contribution ... [T]he clause does not of itself exclude a right to contribution, seeing that the essence of the clause is to apply a rateable liability as a matter of contract. It would therefore be surprising if it had the effect of prejudicing one insurer who had paid too much. Each insurer has not ceased to insure for the same loss just because it cannot be forced by contract to pay more than its rateable proportion or because the clause in effect requires the insured to involve both his insurers at once in order to obtain a full indemnity. In *Legal & General v. Drake* at 161F Lloyd L.J. asked: 'But what is a rateable proportion clause other than an attempt by insurers to exclude the equitable doctrine of contribution by a contractual provision intended to achieve the same effect?' But he did not say that the attempt succeeded. Of course, if the insured is forced to involve both his insurers, then there will be no need for contribution and the need for the application of the doctrine is excluded in fact."

It should be added that in motor insurance cases, which most of these were, the position is further complicated by the existence of statutory rights, vested in an injured third party to enforce judgment fully against the insurer and the right of the insurer to recover that from the person insured (section 151 of the Road Traffic Act 1988; see paragraph 29–26, *post*). In *Legal & General v. Drake*, this was not regarded as affecting the view that the insurer who paid in full was nonetheless a volunteer (see paragraph 23–51, *post*). The court in *Drake v. Provident* was clearly minded to take a different view (see Rix L.J. at paragraph 128 and Pill L.J. at paragraphs 189 and 190).

2. CONTRIBUTION

(c) *Contribution Without Average*

Add to the end of the paragraph as follows:

Policies on property. In *O'Kane v. Jones* [2005] Lloyd's Rep. I.R. 174, **23–50** Richard Siberry Q.C. declined to decide whether the independent liability method or the maximum liability method was the correct approach in a marine insurance case, strictly governed by section 80 of the Marine Insurance Act 1906, because on the facts they produced an identical solution. He did reject, as inconsistent with section 80, an alternative method (the common liability method), under which each insurer would bear equally any loss up to the amount for which each would be independently liable, with the surplus being exclusively borne by the insurer who would be independently liable for that.

Add to the end of the paragraph as follows:

23–51   **Voluntary payment in excess of liability.** However, if the insurers only pay more than they are required to do, in circumstances where they continue to protest their right to contribution from the other insurer, they will not be regarded as making a voluntary payment—*Drake Insurance plc v. Provident Insurance plc* [2004] Q.B. 601, where the Court of Appeal doubted its earlier decision in *Legal and General As. Co. v. Drake Ins. Co.* (footnote 93). See also paragraph 23–27, *ante.*

LIFE INSURANCE

4. CLAIMANT'S TITLE TO POLICY

(b) *Proof of Title*

Add to the end of the paragraph as follows:

Assignee's documents of title. For an example of what was recently **24–39(c)** regarded as reasonable proof of title, see *N M Rothschild & Sons (CI) Ltd v. Equitable Life Ass. Soc.* [2003] Lloyd's Rep. I.R. 370.

7. Trusts and Settled Policies

(4) Settlement Policies under the Provisions of the Married Women's Property Act 1870, s.10 and Married Women's Property Act 1882, s.11

Add to the end of the paragraph as follows:

24–169   By section 70 of the Civil Partnership Act 2004, section 11 applies in relation to a policy of assurance effected by a civil partner on his own life and expressed to be for the benefit of his civil partner, or of his children, or of his civil partner and children, or any of them in the same way as it applies as described above. A civil partnership is a relationship between two people of the same sex that is properly registered under the 2004 Act.

Add new section at end of chapter as follows:

10. Joint Policies

24–260   Where a policy is taken out in joint names, for example those of husband and wife, it may be held by the parties as joint tenants or for their separate interests and it may be important to know whether, on the death of one of them, the policy proceeds belong to the survivor or form part of the deceased's estate. The latter will be the result if a policy held by the parties as joint tenants is severed before the death of the deceased. It is a question of construction of the policy as to which is the correct interpretation. In *Murphy v. Murphy* [2004] Lloyd's Rep. I.R. 744, the issue arose because of a claim made by a dependent of the deceased under the Inheritance (Family Provision) Act 1975, section 9(1) of which permits a claim to a severable share of property held, before the death of the deceased, as a joint tenant.

The policy in question had two elements—a term life insurance element and provision for a payment on terminal illness. A majority of the Court of Appeal held that the life insurance element was not held jointly, as there was a clear inference that the proceeds were to be paid to the survivor, although all the judges regarded the part providing for a terminal illness payment as held jointly. It was important that the life insurance element was pure life insurance with no savings or endowment element, where the natural inference would have been to the contrary.

PERSONAL ACCIDENT POLICIES

3. CAUSATION

General principles. Part of this paragraph was cited in the judgment of the   **25–37**
Court of Appeal in *Blackburn Rovers Football & Athletic Club Ltd v. Avon
Insurance plc* [2005] Lloyd's Rep. I.R. 447, paragraph 11. See paragraph 25–
45, *post.*

Add to the end of the paragraph as follows:
In *Blackburn Rovers Football & Athletic Club Ltd v. Avon Insurance plc*   **25–45**
[2005] Lloyd's Rep. I.R. 447, a preliminary issue arose in respect of a policy
providing cover in respect of accidental bodily injury, which solely and
independently of any other cause occasioned disablement, but which
excluded "permanent total disablement attributable either directly or
indirectly to arthritic or other degenerative conditions, in joints, bones,
muscles, tendons or ligaments." The claimants had obtained the policy to
cover one of their employees, a professional footballer, who suffered an
injury to his back while taking part in a practice match. The injury effectively ended his professional career. The insurers rejected a claim under the
policy on the ground that disablement had not been caused by the injury
alone but resulted directly or indirectly from a degenerative condition of the
lower spine. At first instance, Moore-Bick J. had held that, despite it being

assumed that such a condition was normal for men of the footballer's age, that it was typically exhibited more seriously in top-class professional footballers, that the particular degeneration suffered was no worse than normal for such a footballer of his age and that it was a cause, directly or indirectly, or the injury, the exclusion was to be construed, *inter alia*, as not referring to conditions that were merely a reflection of the normal ageing process. The Court of Appeal held that the exclusion had to be construed as potentially applicable to degeneration experienced by the majority of footballers (although it would still be open on the medical evidence to conclude that the degree of degeneration did not fall within the phrase "arthritic or other degenerative conditions"). It further held that the judge had not applied the proper test of causation. Following *Jason v. Batten*, and distinguishing the "venerable cases" referred to in paragraph 25–37, it was arguable that the degeneration was a proximate cause of the injury and that, because it contained the phrase "attributable either directly or indirectly", the exclusion applied.

4. Particular Clauses

(a) *Clauses Defining Total or Partial Disability*

Add at the end of the first paragraph as follows:

25–49   **Incapacity for any kind of business.** In *Walton v. Airtours plc* [2004] Lloyd's Rep. I.R. 69, the relevant part of the policy effected by an employer for the benefit of its employees, together with the terms and conditions of employment, provided for the payment of benefit if the claimant was "unable to follow any occupation." A former airline pilot suffered from chronic fatigue syndrome and was unable to engage in regular work for a substantial or indefinite period and could not even start any work without structured support, which had not been provided. The Court of Appeal upheld the decision at first instance that benefit was payable, "any occupation" meaning more than a minor or short-term job.

Add new paragraph as follows:

25–51A   **All usual activities.** Modern policies may provide for payment not just if the assured is prevented from following any business, paid work or occupation, but also if he is not in paid employment and is totally disabled from doing all his usual activities. This means all significant non-working activities of a social, sporting, domestic or personal nature which, taken in the round, constitutes so substantial an intrusion on his way of life as to compare with an inability to pursue his normal occupation, if he had had one at the time of the accident or one similar to it—*McGeown v. Direct Travel Insurance* [2004] Lloyd's Rep. I.R. 599.

Add at the end of the second paragraph as follows:

Clauses defining disability. A specific definition of total disablement was in issue in *Howells v. IGI Insurance Co. Ltd* [2003] Lloyd's Rep. I.R. 803. The claimant assured was a professional footballer who, for some years, played for Southampton football club in the English Premier League. The policy insured against total disablement— "the insured's complete and total physical inability to participate in his occupation"—which commenced within 12 months of an accident, but qualified it with a condition stating that if the insured participated in five or more games during the 12 months from the commencement of total disablement, he would be deemed conclusively to have been fully rehabilitated and no claim would be payable. The assured suffered a serious knee injury, following which he never again played for the Southampton first team. However, he played in eight matches for the reserve team following the date of total disablement. It was held that the condition applied and the assured was not eligible to claim under the policy. The assured's occupation was that of professional footballer and "game" meant a game of professional football. There was no reason to read the policy as referring to first team games only. **25–52**

CHAPTER 26

FIRE POLICIES

2. CAUSATION OF LOSS

Add at the end of the paragraph as follows:

Negligence of assured. So, an obligation in a contract to insure against fire **26–27**
is an obligation to insure against fires caused by accident, by the negligence
of the assured or any third party and by the deliberate act of a third party—
Scottish and Newcastle plc v. GD Construction (St Albans) Ltd [2003]
Lloyd's Rep. I.R. 809, 817, 824.

3. PERILS COMMONLY EXCEPTED

Add new n.88a in text after the word "commotion" in line 3:

Insurrections, rebellion, civil war. **26–35**

Add new n.88a:
For an example of a case concerning an exception for "insurrection",
where authorities on the meaning of civil commotion cited in the previous
paragraph were relied on, see the decision of the Court of Appeal for

Trinidad and Tobago in *Grell-Taurel Ltd v. Caribbean Home Insurance Co. Ltd* [2002] Lloyd's Rep. I.R. 655.

Add to the end of the text as follows:

26–40   In *IF P & C Insurance Ltd v. Silversea Cruises Ltd* [2004] Lloyd's Rep. I.R. 696, the Court of Appeal, in the context of a claim under a business interruption policy for losses arising out of the terrorist attacks on the USA on September 11, 2001, commented, *obiter*, on the meaning of the phrases "acts of war" and "armed conflict", indicating that regard would have to be had as to whether business men and their insurers would consider the events as falling within those words of cover. Rix L.J. (at paragraph 143) considered that they were broader than "war" in that they could arise even in the absence of war (which itself might be construed more broadly than in its international law context of armed conflict between sovereign states), and that it might be argued that the events of September 11 could be a cause of war in as much as they led to the invasion of Afghanistan. The fact that everyone could agree that the events were an example of a terrorist attack did not itself answer the question of whether it amounted to something more. On the other hand, Ward L.J. (at paragraph 147) was more cautious, stating that he did not believe that the underwriters and the assured would have regarded the events as acts of war but as terrorist attacks. The "war on terror" declared after those events, was merely a rhetorical response and the war on Afghanistan was a war against that state, not against the organisation responsible for the attacks. He also considered that "armed conflict" must have an air of continuity about it.

CHAPTER 27

OTHER INSURANCES ON PROPERTY

1. BURGLARY AND THEFT

Add at the end of the paragraph as follows:

Technical terms. However, the technical meaning of these terms will not apply where the policy is issued to cover a foreign assured against risks in his jurisdiction—*Canelhas Comercio Importacao E Exportacao Ltd v. Wooldridge* [2004] Lloyd's Rep. I.R. 915. Here the terms will be understood in the sense in which ordinary commercial men would understand them; see paragraph 11–14 *ante*.   **27–1**

2. GOODS IN TRANSIT

Add at the end of the first paragraph as follows:

The decision in *Crow's Transport Ltd v. Phoenix Assurance Co. Ltd* was followed in *Eurodale Manufacturing Ltd v. Ecclesiastical Insurance Office plc* [2003] Lloyd's Rep. I.R. 444, where the typed voyage clause, which in accordance with normal principles prevailed over the printed clauses where they could not be reconciled (see paragraph 11–30, *ante*), provided that cover attached from the time the assured accepted delivery of the insured goods and continued during the ordinary course of transit. This included storage that was an incident of transit.   **27–22**

CHAPTER 28

THIRD PARTY RISKS

1. LIABILITY INSURANCE GENERALLY

(a) *Accrual of Cause of Action*

Add to n.8:

Right to indemnity. See also *Royal & Sun Alliance Ins. plc v. Dornock* **28–2**
[2005] Lloyd's Rep. I.R. 544 at [11] and the decision in *Lumbermen Mutual
Casualty Co. v. Bovis Lend Lease Ltd* [2005] Lloyd's Rep. I.R. 74, where it
was held that a settlement agreement had a different effect from a judgment
or arbitration award. Whereas the latter would normally be conclusive as to
liability and quantum, the settlement of a claim by a third party was not
conclusive as to either. An assured who relied on a settlement as ascertaining
the loss had to prove by extrinsic evidence that he was in truth under a
liability insured by the policy and that what he paid was reasonable, having
regard to the amount of damages that he would have had to pay had the
matter gone to trial. A settlement that failed to identify the loss suffered
specifically by reference to the insured liability could not amount to a valid
ascertainment. No cause of action for an indemnity would arise and no
amount of extrinsic evidence would cause it to do so.

Add to n.17:

28–6   **Legal liability.** An example of where the liability was not covered by the insurance is found in *Frans Maas (U.K.) Ltd v. Sun Alliance and London Ins. Plc* [2004] Lloyd's Rep. I.R. 649. The assured's warehousing business was insured in the following terms:

> "The company will indemnify the insured if the property be damaged during any period of insurance whilst warehoused ... to the extent that there is liability for damage under the contract conditions expressed in the schedule as being insured ..."

It was held that this only covered liability to customers who had contractually engaged the assured's warehousing facilities, not to banks who sued the assured for wrongful interference with goods when the assured had released the goods without production of a bill of lading, in order to assist the customer in repaying a debt to the assured. In acting in this way, the assured was also in breach of a reasonable precautions condition (see para. 28–53, *post*).

(b) *Rights of Third Party Against Insurer*

Delete the last two sentences in the first paragraph and n.36, and replace as follows:

28–11   **Statutory assignment.** The Court of Appeal has now ruled authoritatively on the meaning of "liability" for the purposes of section 1, overruling the decisions in *Tarbuck v. Avon Ins. Co.* (referred to in the deleted sentences) and in *T. & N. Ltd v. Royal & Sun Alliance plc (No. 2)* [2004] Lloyd's Rep. I.R. 106, where it was held that the Act did not apply to liability for a contract debt. In *Re O.T. Computers (In Administration)* [2004] Lloyd's Rep. I.R. 669, the assured, a computer supplier, became insolvent. Many of their customers had purchased computers and extended warranties with credit provided by a finance company. The assured had insured in part against its liability under the warranties with AXA Insurance. The finance company had been obliged to honour claims under the warranties, by virtue of its joint liability under section 75 of the Consumer Credit Act 1974. It claimed to be subrogated to the customers' claims against the insolvent assured and thus potentially to assured's rights against AXA. The action was brought to obtain information about the insurance under section 2 (see paragraph 28–18, *post*). The Court of Appeal rejected the argument that section 1 only applied to liabilities in tort or liabilities arising in tort and contract concurrently and held that liabilities under contracts such as the

92

extended warranties were within the scope of the Act. Longmore L.J. commented at [19]:

> "The words 'Where under any contract of insurance a person ... is insured against liabilities to third parties which he may incur' are perfectly general. To confine 'liabilities' to tortious liabilities or, even, 'tortious liabilities and contractual liabilities akin to tortious liabilities' is to put a considerable gloss upon the statute. Such gloss goes beyond any normally permissible exercise of construction" (at [14]). "These words are perfectly general ... and are apt to include liabilities in debt as much as liabilities in damages".

The fact that an insurance policy might limit its coverage to a liability in damages did not affect the true construction of the Act.

Add to n.32:

In *Re O.T. Computers (In Administration)* [2004] Lloyd's Rep. I.R. 669, which is discussed fully above, the Court of Appeal held that extended warranties provided by the assured were not within s.1(5), so that the assured's arrangements with an insurer to cover their liabilities was not reinsurance and not excluded from the operation of the Act. Longmore L.J. commented at [48] that:

> "[t]he object of section 1(5) was to exclude a right of an insured person to proceed directly against reinsurers in the event of insolvency of an intermediate insurer; although the section does not in terms refer to reinsurance, if [the assured were themselves] insurers of their customers, then their own insurers would effectively be reinsurers."

However, the point was not fully argued and while it seems clear that the extended warranties in the particular case were not contracts of insurance, it is submitted that there may be situations, certainly where they are not provided by the supplier of goods, where they may be—see the discussion at para. 1–9, *ante.*

Add to end of second paragraph as follows:

Liability to be established first. However, the authorities above did not **28–12** directly address the issue as to when the assured's rights are transferred to the third party, that is whether it is on the insolvency of the assured or when liability is established. In *Re O.T. Computers (In Administration)* [2004] Lloyd's Rep. I.R. 669, it was held that the rights are transferred on the occurrence of one of the insolvent events specified in the Act.

"The 1930 Act makes no reference to the need to establish the insured's liability before the transfer takes place. It is therefore more natural to read the Act as envisaging that the transfer to and vesting in the third party of the rights of the insured occurs on insolvency whether the establishment of the right occurs before or after the insolvency. The rights so transferred may be contingent or inchoate in the sense that the rights may not give rise to legal liability on the part of the insurer until the existence and amount of the liability is established but the transfer nevertheless takes place on the insolvency" (*per* Longmore L.J. at [28]).

Support for that view was found in, *inter alia*, the dissenting speech of Lord Templeman in *Bradley v. Eagle Star Ins. Co. Ltd.*, which in this respect was not contradicted by anything in the majority speeches, and in the earlier Court of Appeal decision in *Cox v. Bankside Members Agency Ltd* [1995] 2 Lloyd's Rep. 437 (the judgment of Saville L.J. at 467).

In *Re O.T. Computers (In Administration)*, the point was crucial because of a claim for information under section 2 of the Act (see paragraph 28–18, *post*). The same approach was adopted in the subsequent Court of Appeal decision in *Centre Reinsurance International Co. v. Freakley* [2005] Lloyd's Rep. I.R. 303 (upholding in this respect the judgment at first instance, reported at [2004] Lloyd's Rep. I.R. 22). Here the insolvent assured, which was in administration, was facing a huge quantity of personal injury claims arising from exposure to asbestos. Under a liability policy issued by C, the latter agreed to indemnify the assured in respect of claims in excess of a retained limit of £690m up to a limit of £500m. Until the retained limit was reached, claims were handled by the assured. Between that figure and the limit of £500m, claims were handed by C. C had reinsured its liability under an agreement that contained a claims control clause (see paragraph 33–90, *post*) and the principal issue was whether the reinsurers were entitled under that to take control of the claims against the assured. This in turn depended, *inter alia*, on whether the 1930 Act applied and whether the claims control clause was void under section 1(3) (see paragraph 28–15, *post*). It was held that the Act applied, the statutory transfer having taken place when the assured went into administration, even though there would be third party claimants who, because of the excess and the limit, would have no claims against the insurer.

Add at the end of the paragraph as follows:

28–15   **No contracting out.** In *Centre Reinsurance International Co. v. Freakley* [2005] Lloyd's Rep. I.R. 303, which is described in paragraph 28–12, *ante*, it was held, following the reasoning of the House of Lords, that a claims control clause in a reinsurance agreement did not fall within section 1(3) as it did not purport to alter the rights of the parties under the contract of insurance. The phase "the rights of the parties thereunder" must have been intended to refer only to the rights of the parties in respect of the liability of the insured to the third party which, if altered in the manner for which the contract provides (upon the occurrence of an even giving rise to a statutory transfer) would "cancel, prejudice or reduce" the rights which, under the statute, were to be transferred to the third party "unaltered and undiminished" (*per* Chadwick L.J. at [84] quoting from Lord Goff in *The Fanti*).

Add to n.56:

The view expressed here seems to be supported by Chadwick L.J. in his **28–16**
judgment in *Centre Reinsurance International Co. v. Freakley* [2005] Lloyd's Rep. I.R. 303 at [39 and 40]. However, Arden L.J. ([136] to [139]) took a contrary view. Latham L.J. ([135]) reserved his position as the issue was not the subject of express argument before the court.

Add to n.75:

Duty to give information. These decisions were overruled in *Re O.T.* **28–18**
Computers (In Administration) [2004] Lloyd's Rep. I.R. 669, Longmore L.J., clearly relying on the critique of Sir Jonathan Mance. As explained earlier (see the additional material to para. **28–11**, *ante*), the Court of Appeal held that rights are transferred to the third party under the Act on the occurrence of an appropriate insolvency event. This included the right to information under section 2, which was reasonably required so that the third party could discover whether or not there were rights transferred to him.

(c) *Terms in Liability Policies*

Add at the end of the paragraph as follows:

Notice to insurers. For an example of a notice provision in products lia- **28–24**
bility policies written on a claims made basis, see *Tioxide Europe Ltd v. CGU International Ins. plc* [2005] Lloyd's Rep. I.R. 114.

Add to n.35:

See also *Worsley v. Tambrands Ltd* [2002] Lloyd's Rep. I.R. 382.   **28–42**

Add to n.50:

28-45   **Other words of limitation.** Although the House of Lords ([2003] Lloyd's Rep. I.R. 623) came to a different result (see para. 28–46, *post*), they certainly cast no doubt on this proposition.

Add to n.55:

28-46   See also *Scott v. Copenhagen Reinsurance Co. (U.K.) Ltd* [2003] Lloyd's Rep. I.R. 696 and *Midland Mainline Ltd v. Commercial Union Ass. Co. Ltd* [2004] Lloyd's Rep. I.R. 22 (appeal upheld on other grounds: [2004] Lloyd's Rep. I.R. 739).

Delete the last sentence and n.56 and replace as follows:
In *Lloyds TSB General Holdings v. Lloyds Bank Group Insurance Co. Ltd* [2003] Lloyd's Rep. I.R. 623, a professional indemnity policy provided for the insurers to incur liability only in so far as each and every third party claim exceeded the deductible (£1 million). It further provided:

> "The deductible shall apply to each and every third party claim and shall be subject to no aggregate limitation. If a series of third party claims shall result from any single act or omission (or related series of acts or omissions) then, irrespective of the total number of claims, all such third party claims shall be considered to be a single third party claim for the purposes of the application of the deductible."

The various assureds were faced with a large number of claims based on the mis-selling of personal pensions in respect of which, for the purposes of the present action, they were assumed to have been liable under the rules made by the then regulatory authorities. They had paid compensation exceeding £125 million, but no single claim had exceeded about £35,000, well below the deductible.

Distinguishing the authorities cited earlier in this paragraph, which were concerned with very different wordings of aggregation clauses, the House of Lords held that the claims did not result from a single act or omission or a related series of acts or omissions and thus the assureds did not have an effective claim under the policy. The choice of language used in an aggregation clause was of critical importance. In ascertaining whether or not the claims resulted from a single act or omission, which had to be the proximate cause of the third party claim, it was necessary to examine the cause of action asserted by the third parties. This was the assumed failure of many employees of the assured to give the best advice as required by the regulatory rules. This was not a "single act or omission". The words in parenthesis—"(or related series of acts or omissions)"—did not produce a

different result (in this respect the House of Lords differed from the conclusion reached by the Court of Appeal [2002] Lloyd's Rep. I.R. 113).The
parties could not have meant to have chosen a very narrow unifying factor—an act or omission which gave rise to the civil liability in question—and
then, by a parenthesis, to have produced a clause in which that factor was as
broad as it could be. The acts and omissions of the employees were not a
related series. The words in parenthesis were intended to play a subordinate
role of covering the case in which liability cannot be attributed to a single
act or omission but to the same acts or omissions acting in combination.

Another aggregation issue arose, also in the context of assumed pension
mis-selling, in *Countrywide Assured Group plc v. Marshall* [2003] Lloyd's
Rep. I.R. 195. The policy provided that the liability of the insurers would
not exceed, for any one claim, the sum specified in the schedule and
aggregated claims by defining "any claim" as one occurrence or all occur-
rences of a series consequent upon or attributable to one source or original
cause. However, the relevant deductible or excess was worded to apply to
each and every claimant with no words of aggregation. While Morison J.
recognised that normally the aggregation of claims would apply to both the
aggregate limit and to excesses, he held that the wording used here clearly
imported a different treatment. The assumed mis-selling arose from the lack
of proper training of the assured's sales force and that was one source or
original cause. Therefore, the claims were to be aggregated for the purpose
of the limit of liability, even though the excess would apply to each and
every claimant.

Add to n.60:

Meaning of "claims". In *Mabey & Johnson Ltd v. Ecclesiastical Ins. Office* **28–48**
plc (No. 2) [2004] Lloyd's Rep. I.R. 10, the assured had designed defective
bridges for the state of Ghana under two separate contracts entered into at
different times. In determining whether or not their liability fell under a
"single claim", as provided in the policy, Morrison J. held, following the
decisions in *West Wake Price & Co. v. Ching, Haydon v. Lo & Lo* and
Citibank NA v. Excess Ins. Co. Ltd, supra, that the formulation by the third
party of its claim could not be decisive of the insurers' liability, it was the
underlying facts that were determinative. The claim concerned was not
necessarily one made in legal proceedings. On the contrary, the policy was
looking for the existence of a claim in the policy period made by a third
party against the assured, arising from his alleged negligence. It did not
follow that where there was a separate cause of action, there was a separate
claim. However, on the facts, there were two separate claims as the two
contracts were quite separate and distinct and the design work was not
identical.

Add to n.75:

28–53 **Recklessness required to avoid liability.** For an example of a case where the assured had acted recklessly in breach of a reasonable precautions condition, see *Frans Maas (U.K.) Ltd v. Sun Alliance and London Ins. Plc* [2004] Lloyd's Rep. I.R. 649 (see para. 28–6, *ante*). For a reasonable precautions clause in a products liability policy, see *Tioxide Europe Ltd v. CGU International Ins. plc* [2005] Lloyd's Rep. I.R. 114.

Add new paragraph as follows:

28–58A **Condition regarding sub-contractors.** A public liability policy effected by a contractor may include a condition regarding sub-contractors, requiring the assured to ensure that all sub-contractors to it have employers' liability and public liability insurance in respect of their liability at law. It may further provide that the sub-contractor's policy have a limit of indemnity not less than that under the assured's policy. Such a condition was in issue in *Union Camp Chemicals Ltd v. ACE Insurance SA-NV* [2003] Lloyd's Rep. I.R. 487, where it was contained in a primary liability policy issued by one insurer and was also held to have been incorporated into an excess liability policy issued by a second insurer. Rejecting the argument for the excess liability insurers that the condition required the assured to ensure that every possible sub-contractor it engaged to provide services to it had appropriate insurance, which would not have made commercial sense, it was held that the phrase "all sub-contractors to the insured" had to be construed narrowly and referred only to those sub-contractors who had a legal liability to the assured or to a third party that had given rise to a claim by the assured on its policy. Since on the facts there was such a contractor, a further point arose on the meaning of the second part of the condition. As far as the required limit of indemnity in terms of public liability cover was concerned, the primary policy had a limit of £1 million. The limit in the excess policy was £4 million in excess of £1 million. The relevant sub-contractor had public liability cover of £1 million. It was held that this level of cover satisfied the condition. If any relevant sub-contractor had been required to have a limit of £4 million in excess of £1 million, that would impose an obligation on the assured different and more onerous than that imposed by the primary policy, which only required the assured to ensure that each sub-contractor had cover of £1 million.

(d) *Types of Liability Insurance*

Add to n.88:

A public liability policy covering liability arising from "accidental bodily **28-60** injury" is to be construed from the point of view of the victim, not the assured, so that it will cover liability for injury deliberately inflicted by the assured or someone for whom the latter is variously liable—*Hawley v. Luminar Leisure plc* [2005] Lloyd's Rep. I.R. 275. However, no authorities were referred to by the learned judge and it is perhaps difficult to reconcile this case with decisions such as *Gray v. Barr* [1971] 2 Q.B. 554, discussed in paras. 14-40—14-41 and para. 25-4, *ante*. The claim was brought by the victim under the Third Parties (Rights against Insurers) Act 1930, the assured having been wound up. Had it been a claim made directly by the assured, it would perhaps have failed on public policy grounds.

Add to n.89:

Three further decisions have been reported involving claims under product liability insurance policies. Although the wording was different, in *James Budgett Sugars Ltd v. Norwich Union Ins. Ltd* [2003] Lloyd's Rep. I.R. 110, the court in effect reached the same result as in *A S Screenprint Ltd v. British Reserve Ins. Co. Ltd* and *Rodan v. Commercial Union Ass. Co. plc*. The assured had supplied contaminated sugar to a customer to be used in the manufacture of mincemeat. The assured admitted that it was in breach of contract to the customer but denied liability for consequential loss of business suffered by the customer. The issue was whether, assuming the assured was liable for such losses, it would be entitled to an indemnity from its liability insurer. The policy provided for insurance "in the event of accidental personal injury or loss of or damage (defined as physical damage) to property (defined as material property)" and continued "in respect of such an event, the [insurer] will provide indemnity against legal liability". It was held that, despite its inelegance, the wording was not apt to cover liability for consequential losses; the words "in respect of such an event" were included to limit the scope of the indemnity to liability in respect of physical loss or damage.

A similar result was reached in *Pilkington United Kingdom plc v. CGU Ins. plc* [2004] Lloyd's Rep. I.R. 891. Here the claimant assured, as sub-contractor, had supplied toughened glass panels in the roof and vertical panelling of the Eurostar terminal at Waterloo station. A small number of the panels proved defective in that they fractured after installation. They were not replaced, but instead Eurostar installed safety features to prevent any glass falling on members of the public or staff. No personal injury was caused, nor was there any damage to the fabric of the terminal other than the panels themselves. The main contractor claimed a contribution from the assured in respect of their liability to Eurostar for the costs of investigation and the remedial works. The assured settled this claim, recovered some of its liability from other insurers and claimed the balance from the defendant insurers under their products liability cover with them. The policy provided indemnity against all liability of the assured in respect of any occurrence to which the policy applied as stated in the specification. The relevant part of the specification provided:

"Products liability — (a) Bodily injury or illness or disease ... (b) Loss of or physical damage to physical property not belonging to the insured ... caused by any commodity, article or thing supplied, installed, erected, repaired, altered or treated by the insured ..."

The policy contained two relevant "particular clauses". Clause 6, headed "Contractual Liability (Product)", provided that the policy would not apply to liability assumed by the insured by agreement in respect of injury, etc. caused by any commodity, article or thing supplied, installed or erected by the insured unless such liability would have attached in the absence of such agreement. Clause 16, headed "Damage to Goods Supplied", provided that the policy would not apply to liability in respect of recalling, removing, repairing, replacing, reinstating or the cost of or reduction in value of any commodity, article or thing supplied, etc. if such liability arose from any defect therein or the harmful nature or unsuitability thereof. The Court of Appeal held that the assured's claim failed on the ground that the loss was not within the policy wording (there was also a breach of condition precedent by the assured). Following *A S Screenprint Ltd v. British Reserve Ins. Co. Ltd*, *Rodan v. Commercial Union Ass. Co. plc* and *James Budgett Sugars Ltd v. Norwich Union Ins. Ltd*, it was clear that, in order to establish cover, the assured,

"must demonstrate some physical damage caused by the commodity for which purpose a defect or deterioration in the commodity itself is not sufficient and that the loss claimed must be a loss resulting from physical loss or damage to physical property of another (or some personal injury)" (*per* Potter L.J. at [35]).

There was no basis for holding that physical damage had occurred to the building simply by the incorporation of a defective component. Provided that the building functioned effectively, to take precautions against the possibility of some future problem was to anticipate damage covered by the policy and the cost of such measures was not covered without specific provision. "Damage" usually referred to a changed physical state and the policy expressly required physical damage to the property of another.

Rather different policy wording was the subject of *Tioxide Europe Ltd v. CGU International Ins. plc* [2005] Lloyd's Rep. I.R. 114. The claimant assured had manufactured and supplied a pigment that was used by the manufacturers of white u-PVC products. It was assumed that, because of a defect in the pigment, u-PVC products had become discoloured in certain conditions and that the assured was liable to their buyers for the economic loss and damage suffered by them as a result. The insurance was arranged in three layers, the relevant terms providing that the insurers would indemnify the assured against liability assumed under contract or agreement for damages "on account of" property damage resulting from each loss, but only such damage that was neither expected nor intended by the assured. Property damage was defined as (a) physical injury to or destruction of tangible property including the loss of use thereof resulting therefrom and (b) loss of use of tangible property which had not been physically injured or destroyed, in both cases to property not owned by the assured. Loss was defined as "an accident, including continuous or repeated exposure to the same general harmful conditions." The key issues for decision, apart from whether or not the assured had complied with notice requirements in the policy (not considered in detail here) were (1) whether the claims against the assured were within the cover provided and (2) whether there was a single loss arising out of the various claims that had been made. This went to the question of whether the primary and excess layer policies were to respond, depending on the various sums insured and deductibles. It was held that, although the claims against the assured were for economic loss and not for damage to property, the words "on account of" physical injury were sufficiently wide to encompass claims for the cost of repair or replacement of products that had become discoloured. This was broader than claims "for" or "in respect of" property damage. However, claims for loss of business or profits arising from discolourisation could not be said to be claims "on account of" physical injury to the finished products. As far as the second issue was concerned, there was no single loss—there was no unifying event that led to the individual cases of discolourisation. The original cause of that, the error of supplying a defective pigment, was not an accident or a continuous and repeated exposure to the same general harmful conditions.

2. PROFESSIONAL INDEMNITY POLICIES

Add to n.7:

Whether cover for non-negligent act. See also *Lumbermen Mutual Casualty* **28–63** *Co. v. Bovis Lend Lease Ltd* [2005] Lloyd's Rep. I.R. 74, where Colman J. held that "error or omission" in the phrase "any neglect error or omission" could cover non-negligent conduct giving rise to liability.

Add to end of the paragraph as follows:

28–83   The decision in *Friends Provident Life and Pensions Ltd v. Sirius International Ins. Corp.* [2005] Lloyd's Rep. 135 was concerned with a number of issues regarding notification arising out of professional indemnity insurance being arranged in layers. The primary layer policy had a clause to the same effect as that considered above. The leading excess layer policy had a similar clause, but the other excess layer policies did not. However, there policies had a clause under which they were stated to be subject to the same terms and conditions as the "co-insurance" policies. Recognising that it was the general practice of the insurance market to (1) write professional indemnity risks on a "claims made" basis (see paragraph 28–85, *post*) with an extension to cover losses notified in the policy period and (2) to insure large risks by means of primary and excess layer policies where, in the absence of any indication to the contrary, the scope of the excess layer is intended to be the same, apart from with regard to policy limits, as that provided under the primary layer, Moore-Bick J. held that the notification clause was incorporated into the excess layer policies. Further, notice to the primary layer insurers under the clause was sufficient notice to the excess layer insurers, although the term in the primary layer insurance, conferring authority to receive notice on the brokers, was not so incorporated as this was not germane to the risk and was purely a matter of administration.

3. EMPLOYERS' LIABILITY POLICIES

Add to n.51:

28–87   **Compulsion to insure.** A further exemption was introduced by the Employers' Liability (Compulsory Insurance) Amendment Regulations 2004 (S.I. 2004 No. 2882), with effect from February 28, 2005, namely, for any employer which is a company with only one employee who also owns fifty per cent or more of the issued share capital in that company.

CHAPTER 29

MOTOR VEHICLE INSURANCE

Add at the end of the paragraph as follows:

The provisions of Directive 2000/26/E.C. (see footnote 8) have been **29–1** introduced in various pieces of secondary legislation, as described in the following and in subsequent paragraphs. The Motor Vehicles (Compulsory Insurance) (Information Centre and Compensation Body) Regulations 2003, (S.I. 2003 No. 37), established the Motor Insurers' Information Centre ("M.I.I.C.") in order to assist persons to seek compensation occurring in an EEA State other than their State of Residence. M.I.I.C must keep, in respect of motor vehicles normally based in the UK, the name and address of the insurer and the number of the insurance policy (regulation 4) and has the right to require insurers to supply it with the requisite information (regulations 5 and 6). A person injured or whose property is damaged in a motor accident, who is resident in an EEA State, can require M.I.I.C. to supply him with insurance details where the accident occurs in the UK, or where the vehicle is usually based in the UK and the accident occurs in the EEA or a state subscribing to the Green Card scheme, or where he resides in the UK and the accident occurs in one of those states (regulation 9).

(a) *Risks Covered*

Add to n.18:

29–3   **Using and causing or permitting use.** See also *Bretton v. Hancock* [2005] Lloyd's Rep. I.R. 454.

Add to n.40:

29–5   **Essentials of valid policy.** Additional requirements have been imposed pursuant to the Fourth Motor Insurance Directive (Directive 2000/26/E.C.). Under the Financial Services and Markets Act 2000 (Fourth Motor Insurance Directive) Regulations 2002 (S.I. 2002 No. 2706), rules made by the Financial Services Authority may require authorised motor insurers to make interest payments in certain circumstances. Under the Financial Services and Markets Act (Variation of Threshold Conditions) Order 2002 (S.I. 2002 No. 2707), such insurers must have a claims representative in each EEA State other than the UK, namely a person with responsibility for handling and settling claims arising from accidents when insurance is compulsory.

Add to n.42:
"Arising out of the use of the vehicle" does not cover the situation where a vehicle has stopped to pick up a passenger who is injured when crossing the road in an attempt to reach the vehicle (*Slater v. Buckinghamshire County Council* [2004] Lloyd's Rep. I.R. 432), although it can cover the case of someone who leaves their vehicle parked having run out of petrol and, when crossing the road to get help, causes an accident (*Dunthorne v. Bentley* [1999] Lloyd's Rep. I.R. 560).

(b) *Policy "In Force"*

Add to n.64:
29–6   See also *Lloyd-Wolper v. Moore* [2004] Lloyd's Rep. I.R. 730 (see further para. 29–26, *post*).

(c) *Persons Entitled to Indemnity or Compensation from Motor Insurers*

Add at the end of the paragraph as follows:

29–22   **Claims by third parties not specified in the policy.** A further right has been vested in third parties, as described in paragraph 29–38A, *post*. As to the right of third parties to obtain information about motor insurance from the Motor Insurers' Information Centre, see paragraph 29–1, *ante*.

Add at the end of the paragraph as follows:

Insurer's rights of recovery. "Permitted" bears the same meaning as it does **29–26** under section 143 (see paragraphs 29–3 and 29–6, *ante*)—*Lloyd-Wolper v. Moore* [2004] Lloyd's Rep. I.R. 730. So there is liability under section 151(7) where there is an honest, although mistaken belief as to the circumstances of the person to whom permission was given, for example that he had a valid licence to drive.

Add to n.63:

Notice of bringing of proceedings. A legal secretary employed by solicitors **29–28** acting for the insurers can have authority to receive notice—*Nawaz v. Crowe Insurance Group* [2003] Lloyd's Rep. I.R. 471. See also the comments made by Kennedy L.J. as to the importance of formal notice at para. 26.

Add new paragraph as follows:

Alternative right for third party to sue insurers. There is now an alternative **29–38A** way in which third parties may proceed, introduced by the European Communities (Rights against Insurers) Regulations 2002 (S.I. 2002 No. 3061). These were in force from January 19, 2003, seemingly irrespective of the date on which the accident occurred. These regulations implement part of the EC Fourth Directive (Directive 2000/26/E.C.), but in fact go further than that Directive requires. The critical point is that, subject to the requirements explained below, a third party may proceed directly against the insurers without first having to obtain a judgment against the negligent driver, although the insurers will be able to defend the claim on the basis that the driver was not in fact liable in tort. The regulations provide that an "entitled party" can, without prejudice to his right to issue proceedings against the insured person, issue proceedings against the insurer, which "shall be directly liable to the entitled party to the extent that he is liable to the insured person" (regulation 3(2)). An entitled party is someone who is a resident of the UK or any other EEA Member State (regulation 2(1)), so, for example, a visitor from outside Europe is unable to use this right.

In addition, the entitled person must have a cause of action in tort against an "insured person", which arises out of an accident caused by or arising out of the use of a vehicle on a road or other public place in the UK and the vehicle must be normally based in the UK. For these purposes an insured person is a person insured under a policy fulfilling the requirements of section 145 of the 1988 Act (see paragraph 29–5, *ante*). The requirement for an "accident" is not one that appears anywhere else in the compulsory motor insurance requirements. Theoretically, it could limit the application of the right, or at least raise the issue of whether or not a deliberate or reckless running down could be regarded as an accident (this question is considered in Chapter 14, *ante*). In practice, it seems unlikely to matter, since under the regulations the victim has no better rights than the insured, and it is clear that, on public policy grounds, the insured would not be entitled to an indemnity in such a case. In contrast, public policy would not prevent an action brought under section 151 of the 1988 Act. There are other limits to this right, in contrast to the position under section 151. While the restrictions in section 148 would also apply to an action brought under the Regulations, there is no other restriction on the insurer's contractual rights. There is no right under the Regulations to sue in respect of a tort committed by someone not insured under the policy nor when the insurance has actually been cancelled. In the latter case, section 151 will still apply if the insured is in possession of the certificate of insurance.

Delete the last six lines of the paragraph and replace as follows:

29–39   **The Motor Insurers' Bureau: The two agreements.** The agreement regarding untraced drivers was replaced by one dated June 14, 1996 and then by one dated February 7, 2003. Although first agreed long before the E.C. Second Motor Insurance Directive (84/5/EEC), they have subsequently been recognised as implementing the requirements thereof. The issue of whether this was a sufficient implementation was referred to the European Court of Justice (n.5), which, in *Evans v. Secretary of State for the Environment, Transport and the Regions*, Case C-63/01, [2004] Lloyd's Rep. I.R. 391, confirmed that it was. The M.I.B. has now received further statutory recognition in that certain claimants have a right to claim compensation from it (see paragraph 29–52, *post*) and it is the official compensation body for the UK for the purposes of the fourth Motor Insurance Directive (The Motor Vehicles (Compulsory Insurance) (Information Centre and Compensation Body) Regulations 2003, (S.I. 2003 No. 37), regulation 10).

Add at the end of the paragraph as follows:

29–46   **"Ought to have known".** This construction was applied in a further case on the 1988 Agreement—*Akers v. Motor Insurers' Bureau* [2003] Lloyd's Rep. I.R. 427. Here the victim was unable to recover when he had information from which he realised that the driver might well not be insured, but deliberately refrained from asking questions. In *Pickett v. Motor Insurers' Bureau* [2004] Lloyd's Rep. I.R. 513, the principal issue was whether or not the victim was "allowing himself to be carried in or upon the vehicle". The victim had entered the vehicle as a passenger knowing that the driver was uninsured, but when the latter started doing handbrake turns on a narrow track (something that he had done before when the victim was in the vehicle), she asked him to stop so that she could get out. It was held that, once she had given consent to being carried, it could only be withdrawn by an unequivocal repudiation of the common venture to which the consent had been given when she entered the vehicle. The relevant part of the clause was aimed at persons consciously colluding in the use of an uninsured vehicle.

Add at the end of the first paragraph as follows:

Untraced drivers. A further agreement with the same title of February 7, 2003, applies to accidents occurring on or after February 14, 2003. This is considered in new paragraph 29–51A, *post,* so paragraphs 29–48 to 29–51 should be read as applicable only to cases covered by the 1996 Agreement. **29–47**

Delete sentence after n.57 and replace as follows:

Amount payable. Under the former Agreement, interest was not payable on an award, and the question of whether this was compatible with the second Motor Insurance Directive was referred to the European Court of Justice. In *Evans v. Secretary of State for the Environment, Transport and the Regions*, Case C-63/01, [2004] Lloyd's Rep. I.R. 391, the European Court of Justice decided that Member States should lay down the rules to ensure adequate compensation, implying that interest ought to be provided for, but this is academic in respect of claims under the 2003 Agreement, which now expressly (clause 9) requires the M.I.B. to pay interest. **29–49**

Add new paragraphs as follows:

The 2003 untraced drivers' agreement. The 2003 Agreement is, like the earlier 1996 Agreement, rather complex and we do not give a full account here. In particular, we do not consider the detailed procedures laid down for handling the claim, investigations and reports, the making of payments and appeals, which are broadly the same as under the 1996 Agreement and as described in paragraph 29–51, *ante*. It is important to note that, whereas the 1996 and earlier Agreements did not cover claims for property damage, these are now allowed, subject to an excess of £300, in certain situations (clauses 4 and 5) but not, (i) when there is no claim for compensation in respect of death or bodily injury, (ii) if the property was insured and the applicant has recovered the full amount of his loss from an insurer nor (iii) in the case of damage to a motor vehicle, if the vehicle was not compulsorily **29–51A**

insured to the knowledge of the person suffering the damage. A significant change from the earlier agreement is the provisions that allow the payment of interest and costs (clauses 9 and 10). A number of requirements must be satisfied by an applicant for an award (clause 4), including:

(1) The applicant must be unable to trace the person responsible for the death, injury or damage or a person partly so responsible.
(2) The death, injury or damage must have been caused in circumstances such that on the balance of probabilities, the untraced person would have been liable to the applicant in damages.
(3) That liability must have been one required to be insured against under the 1988 Act; this is assumed in the absence of evidence to the contrary.
(4) The application must be made in writing within three years of the accident for personal injury claims (nine months for property damage claims).

There are exceptions (clause 5) that are very similar to the exceptions in the earlier Agreement, including claims from passengers involved in a crime (this is subject to knowledge on the same basis as in the Uninsured Drivers Agreement—see paragraph 29–46, *ante*). Injury or loss resulting from terrorist acts is also excluded. The amount of compensation awarded to the applicant, is assessed on the same basis as a court would assess damages in a tort action, except that the M.I.B. does not award damages for loss of earnings in so far as they have been paid by the applicant's employer (clause 8).

There are special provisions (clauses 12 to 15) dealing with the cases where an untraced driver was only partly to blame for the accident. Here the applicant may be required to obtain judgment against the known driver or the known principal of an unidentified driver, or the applicant may have obtained such judgment without being required to do so. If this judgment is not satisfied within three months, the M.I.B. awards an amount equal to the untraced person's contribution to a full award, namely, that proportion which a court would have awarded if proceedings had been taken against all the tortfeasors. If this judgment is only partly satisfied within three months, the M.I.B. awards an amount equal to either the unsatisfied part of the judgment or the untraced person's contribution, whichever is the greater. If the applicant has not obtained, and is not required by the M.I.B. to obtain, judgment against the known driver, and has not received any payment as compensation from any such person, the amount the M.I.B. awards is an amount equal to the untraced person's contribution to a full award.

Clause 11 specifies conditions precedent to the liability of the M.I.B., including, (1) that the applicant must give all such assistance as the M.I.B. reasonably requires, to enable any necessary investigation to be carried out; (2) if required, that the applicant must take all reasonable steps to obtain judgment against any person or persons in respect of their liability to the applicant; this is subject to his being indemnified against costs by the M.I.B.; and (3) if required, that the applicant must assign to the M.I.B., or their nominee, any judgment obtained by him; if this produces a surplus over what the M.I.B. paid the applicant, the M.I.B. is accountable for this after deducting the reasonable expenses of the recovery of the sum for which the judgment was given. If required to do so, the applicant must furnish a statutory declaration concerning the facts and circumstances upon which his claim is based.

Add at the end of the paragraph as follows:

M.I.B. as party to litigation. As the current untraced drivers' agreement **29–52** was agreed after the Contracts (Rights of Third Parties) Act 1999 came into force (see footnote 68), an injured claimant might now have a statutory right to sue the M.I.B. under that agreement. Further, certain claimants now have a right to claim compensation from the M.I.B. under the Motor Vehicles (Compulsory Insurance) (Information Centre and Compensation Body) Regulations 2003, (S.I. 2003 No. 37), implementing part of the fourth Motor Insurance Directive.

To have a right under the Regulations in respect of an insured vehicle, the claimant must be resident in the UK, the accident must have occurred in an EEA State other than the UK or in a country subscribing to the Green Card Scheme and the vehicle whose use caused the injury or damage must normally be based and insured in an EEA State other than the UK. The claimant must have sought compensation from the insurer or his claims representative, which has failed to make a reasoned reply within three months, and must not have commenced legal proceedings against the insurer (regulation 11). On receipt of a claim, the M.I.B. must immediately notify (i) the insurer or their claims representative; (ii) the foreign compensation body in the State in which that insurer is established and (iii) if known, the person who caused the accident that it has received a claim and will respond to it within two months of receipt, and it must respond to the claimant within that two months. If the M.I.B. is satisfied by the claimant that the person who caused the accident is liable to the claimant and as to the amount of loss and damage (including interest) that is properly recoverable in consequence of that accident, under the laws applying in that part of the UK in which the claimant resided at the date of the accident, the M.I.B. must indemnify the claimant in respect of the loss and damage. The M.I.B. must cease to act in response to a claim as soon as it becomes aware that the insurer or its claims representative has made a reasoned response, or the claimant has commenced legal proceedings against the insurer (regulation 12).

Where someone has suffered loss or injury and it has proved impossible to identify the vehicle, the use of which is alleged to have been responsible for the accident or, within two months after the date of the request, to identify an insurer insuring the use of the vehicle, an injured party resident in the UK can claim compensation from the M.I.B. if the accident, caused by or arising out of the use of a vehicle which is normally based in an EEA State, occurred on the territory of a EEA State other than the UK or a State subscribing to the Green Card Scheme and he has made a request for information from the Motor Insurers' Information Centre. The M.I.B. must then treat the case as governed by the untraced drivers' agreement (regulation 13). As to provisions regarding the M.I.B. having to compensate its equivalents in other EEA states, see regulations 14 and 15.

(d) Breach of Duty to Insure

Add at the end of the first paragraph, after n.91 as follows:

29–55 **Common law remedy.** That a claim under this principle for damages where someone is injured or killed is a claim for personal injuries and does not comprehend a claim for pure economic loss, was confirmed in *Bretton v. Hancock* [2005] Lloyd's Rep. I.R. 454. Here the claimant B had an ownership interest in the vehicle being driven by her uninsured fiancé, in which she was a passenger. An accident for which the latter was found 25 per cent to blame and the other driver 75 per cent, caused the death of the fiancé and injury to the other driver, the defendant H, who brought a counterclaim against B for breach of statutory duty. It was held that although B had been using the car within the meaning of section 143, a user was not bound to insure against the liability of one tortfeasor to contribute with another tortfeasor in respect of their joint liability to the user. As the Road Traffic Act was only concerned with third party risks, the principle operated only when the victim was the claimant and there was an essential difference between the claim of the primary victim and claim of the joint tortfeasor which was only in respect of the other tortfeasor's right of indemnity or contribution.

(e) Terms and Conditions of Motor Policies

Add to n.28:

29–67 **Dual purposes.** See also *Keeley v. Pashen* [2005] Lloyd's Rep. I.R. 289 and, for the application of the same principle in a marine policy, *Caple v. Sewell* [2002] Lloyd's Rep. I.R. 626.

Add at the end of the paragraph as follows:

Use for hiring. However, this condition does not apply where the assured   **29–68**
is driving home after his last fare-paying passengers of the day have left the
vehicle—*Keeley v. Pashen* [2005] Lloyd's Rep. I.R. 289.

CHAPTER 30

AVIATION INSURANCE

Delete the second sentence — **30–2**

Add new paragraphs as follows:

Insurance in respect of liability in respect of passengers, baggage, cargo **30–2A** and third parties is now compulsory under Regulation 785/04 of the European Parliament and Council (April 21, 2004, O.J. L138), as supplemented by the Civil Aviation (Insurance) Regulations 2005, (S.I. 2005 No. 1089), (the latter are primarily concerned with the enforcement mechanisms). The Regulation applies to all air carriers and aircraft operators flying within, into, out of or over the territory of a Member State (article 2(1)). There are exemptions for state aircraft, model aircraft below a specified size, foot-launched flying machines, captive balloons, kites and parachutes. There is no requirement for insurance against war risks or terrorism in respect of aircraft, including gliders, with a maximum take off mass of less than 500 kilograms, and microlights used for non-commercial purposes or local flight instruction which does not entail the crossing of international borders (article 2(2)). The insured risks must include acts of war, terrorism, hijacking, acts of sabotage, unlawful seizure of aircraft and civil commotion (article 4(1)).

Article 6 specifies the minimum cover for passengers, baggage and cargo. Insurance against liability in respect of passengers must be at least 250,000 special drawing rights ("S.D.R") per passenger (although a lower level of 100,000 S.D.R.s is permissible (and has been followed in the UK Regulations) for non-commercial operations by aircraft with a maximum take off mass of 2,700 kilograms or less). Liability in respect of baggage must be a minimum of 1,000 S.D.R.s per passenger and in respect of cargo, 17 S.D.R.s per kilogram. The S.D.R. is the unit of account of the International Monetary Fund and is currently worth approximately £1.75.

The minimum cover in respect of liability to third parties must be per accident for each and every aircraft. Article 7 lays down a table under which the amount varies according to the maximum take off mass of aircraft. This should be consulted for the detail, but in brief the requirements range from a minimum of 750,000 S.D.R.s for aircraft with a maximum take off mass of less than 500 kilograms to a minimum of 700,000,000 for aircraft with a maximum take off mass of 500,000 kilograms or more.

Add to n.5:

30–3   **Standard policies.** See also *Scott v. Copenhagen Reinsurance Co. (UK) Ltd* [2003] Lloyd's Rep. I.R. 696 at [22].

30–4   *Add new n.9a in text at the end of the first sentence:*

Add new n.9a:

For discussion of the meaning of war risks in a business interruption policy, see *IF P & C Insurance Ltd v. Silversea Cruises* Ltd [2004] Lloyd's Rep. I.R. 696, para. 26–40, *ante*.

CHAPTER 31

INSURANCE AGAINST PECUNIARY LOSS

1. CONSEQUENTIAL LOSS INSURANCE

Add to n.4:

Loss of profits. For a case concerning loss of income following the ter-   **31–1**
rorist attacks in the USA on September 11, 2001, see *IF P & C Insurance Ltd
v. Silversea Cruises Ltd* [2004] Lloyd's Rep. I.R. 696. As with any other
indemnity policy, the proximate cause of the loss must not be an excluded
peril (see ch.19). For recent cases applying the doctrine to consequential loss
insurances, see *IF P & C Insurance Ltd v. Silversea Cruises Ltd*, above,
Midland Mainline Ltd v. Eagle Star Ins. Co. Ltd [2004] Lloyd's Rep. 739 and
Tektrol Ltd v. International Ins. Co. of Hanover Ltd [2005] Lloyd's Rep. I.R.
358.

Add to n.9:

Measure of indemnity. In *Normhurst Ltd v. Dornoch Ltd* [2005] Lloyd's   **31–2**
Rep. I.R. 27, it was held that a claim under a consequential loss policy is a
claim for damages and governed by the principle that there is no further
claim for damages based on the insurer's unjustified refusal to pay a valid
claim (see paras. 19–70, *ante*).

2. CREDIT INSURANCE

Add to n.59:

31–16   **Nature of the risk**. See also *Moore Large & Co. Ltd v. Hermes Credit & Guarantee plc* [2003] Lloyd's Rep. I.R. 315.

Add at the end of the paragraph as follows:

31–20   **Non-disclosure of material facts.** When increased cover has been requested, the assured should disclose a high level of trading with the debtor outside the peak period for which that cover has been requested—*Moore Large & Co. Ltd v. Hermes Credit & Guarantee plc* [2003] Lloyd's Rep. I.R. 315, although on the facts the insurer had waived the non-disclosure and affirmed the policy.

Add at the end of the paragraph as follows:

31–21   **Measure of liability.** A policy insuring against the failure of a particular customer of the assured will contain a credit limit which serves as the limit of the insurer's liability. In *Moore Large & Co. Ltd v. Hermes Credit & Guarantee plc* [2003] Lloyd's Rep. I.R. 315, the relevant policy wording provided that the amount of loss in respect of which the policy provided an indemnity was such amount of "qualifying debt" as should not exceed the credit limit and as should be admitted to rank in the insolvent estate of the customer. "Qualifying debt" was such amount of "qualifying invoice" as should remain unpaid after the due date. It was held that this related to losses at the date of insolvency. The insurers were not simply insuring debts attributable to such invoices as were within the credit limit at the time when they were issued.

4. INSURANCE DISTINGUISHED FROM SURETYSHIP

Add to n.83:

31–46   The approach of the Court of Appeal was left undisturbed by the House of Lords— [2002] UKHL 28, and has subsequently been followed in *Re Claims Direct Test Cases* [2003] Lloyd's Rep. I.R. 677. Here an organisation called Claims Direct provided services additional to the insurance cover that they procured on behalf of their customers through Lloyd's brokers. Affirming the approach of Chief Master Hurst ([2003] Lloyd's Rep. I.R. 69), the Court of Appeal held that the proper approach was to identify the amount that customers were charged that was properly the premium for the insurance and only that amount was recoverable.

CHAPTER 32

CONTRACTORS' RISKS POLICIES

Add to n.2:

Contractor's risks. For recent Court of Appeal decisions considering the   **32–1**
scope of insurance obligations under construction contracts, see *Skanska
Construction Ltd v. Egger (Barony) Ltd* [2003] Lloyd's Rep. I.R. 479 and
Scottish and Newcastle plc v. GD Construction (St Albans) Ltd [2003]
Lloyd's Rep. I.R. 809.

Add to n.32:

Contractors' liability. The construction of a standard condition was in   **32–14**
issue in *Cornhill Insurance plc v. D E Stamp Felt Roofing Contractors Ltd*
[2002] Lloyd's Rep. I.R. 648. Here the assured was required to arrange for
specified precautions to be taken whenever work was carried out involving
the application of heat. This was held only to require the setting up of a
system and did not amount to a guarantee that the system would work.

Add new paragraphs as follows:

Damage to property. While the liability insurance section of a contractor's   **32–17A**
policy will usually provide cover against damage to property, it will normally exclude liability in respect of damage to property belonging to the
insured and damage to the defective part of any product supplied or contract works, or the costs or expenses incurred in repairing, replacing,
recalling or making any refund in respect of the defective part of any product supplied or contract works. In *James Longley & Co. v. Forest Giles Ltd*
[2002] Lloyd's Rep. I.R. 421, the assured contracted with the claimant, the
main contractor in the construction of a new building to lay vinyl flooring,
but the screed laid underneath was not allowed to dry out properly and as a

result the adhesive for the flooring did not cure properly. The claimant had to incur the costs of remedial works and was additionally liable to the employer for damages because the project was completed late. The question was whether the assured's liability to the claimant fell within its policy, which contained the standard wording above. It was held that neither the costs of remedial works nor the damages paid by the claimant were covered. It was not the usual intention, in a contractor's public liability insurance, to give cover in respect of defective workmanship that did not cause physical damage to the personal property of a third party or interference with their property rights, as opposed to their purely economic interests. Even if there were damage to property, it was only to the surface of the vinyl and possibly the screed, which was either a product supplied by the assured or which formed part of their contract works. The damages payable by the claimant were not based on damage to property and the fact that the policy defined damage to include loss did not mean that damage was incurred where, as the consequence of an insured event, a third party was left financially poorer than he was before. In this context, loss meant simply loss of property so that this as well as damage was covered.

For a further example of damage to property, in a case concerning the construction of a Belgian policy, see *Jan de Nul (UK) Ltd v. Axa Royale Belge S.A.* [2002] Lloyd's Rep. I.R. 589.

CHAPTER 33

REINSURANCE

Add to n.44:

Cession, acceptance and retention. A retention warranty must be clearly **33–12**
expressed. In *GE Re. v. New Hampshire Ins. Co* [2004] Lloyd's Rep. I.R. 404,
a stipulation that "Ceding Company retains 20% (with reinsurance)" was
construed in its context to do no more than show that 20% of the cedant's
line was not being reinsured, and there was no bar on it reinsuring that part
of its exposure. The *Kingscroft* case was distinguished.

Add new sub-paragraphs as follows:

Fronting. If the reason for interposing insurer B is that C, the original **33–21**
assured, has doubts concerning A's solvency, B will have to decide how best
to ensure that A will indemnify him in the event of a claim by C. One
method commonly used is to insist upon the establishment by A of a
banker's letter of credit on which B can draw for reimbursement after
having paid a claim made by C. Typically, the bank will require cash col-
lateral to be deposited by A—*Ludgate Insurance Co v. Citibank NA* [1998]
Lloyd's Rep. I.R. 221. The importance of clearly defining the circumstances
in which B is entitled to draw down on the letter of credit, is demonstrated
by *Sirius International Insurance Co (Publ) v. FAI General Insurance Ltd*
[2005] 1 All E.R. (Comm) 117. Here these were clearly set out when the credit
was established, but difficulties were created by the wording of a Tomlin
order by which arbitration proceedings started by B against A were settled,
and the resulting dispute was ultimately resolved by the House of Lords.
In *North Atlantic Insurance Co. v. Nationwide General Insurance Co.*
[2004] 2 All E.R. (Comm) 351, one of the pool members acted as a 100%
front for the other pool members. The pool went into run-off. The fronting
company remained solvent, but two other pool members became insolvent.
The fronter claimed direct access to the reinsurance recoveries received from

the pool's reinsurers, because it was responsible for the insolvent members' shares of the pool's overall liabilities, but could not recover a full indemnity from them. The claim failed. The managing agent of the pool had concluded the reinsurances on behalf of all pool members, on the basis that each contributed to the premium and each was entitled to a share of the recoveries corresponding to its share of pool liabilities. The reinsurers were not parties to the fronting arrangement. Nothing prevented the liquidators of the insolvent pool members from collecting their share of the recoveries for the benefit of these members' general creditors. It would have been possible to establish a trust over the pool's reinsurance proceeds but this had not been done. Any attempt to create special accounting arrangements governing distribution of these proceeds to operate in the event of insolvency of one or more pool members, would in any case have run foul of the rule of public policy in *British Eagle International v. Cia. Nationale Air France* [1975] 1 W.L.R. 758.

Add to n.75:

33–23   **Subject matter and interest.** In *Toomey v. Banco Vitalicio de Espana* [2005] Lloyd's Rep. 423, 433, Thomas L.J. described reinsurance as the insurance of an insurable interest in the subject matter of an original insurance, following *Toomey v. Eagle Star* [1994] 2 Lloyd's Rep. 516, 522.

Add at the end of the paragraph:

33–26   **The slip.** There is no reason why the parties to a reinsurance should not intend that, before being unconditionally bound, a written contract will be executed. The wording of the contract may well be complex and require careful negotiation. In such a case one must therefore distinguish between a party's agreement on the wording itself, and his assent to be bound by the contract once it is executed—*Sun Life Assurance Co of Canada v. CX Reinsurance Co Ltd.* [2004] Lloyd's Rep. I.R. 58, citing *New England Reinsurance Corp. v. Messoghios Insurance Co.* [1992] 2 Lloyd's Rep. 251, 255.

Add to n.92:

33–27   **Characteristics of reinsurance slips.** *Bonner v. Cox Dedicated Corporate Member Ltd* [2005] Lloyd's Rep. I.R. 569 *per* Morison J.

Add to the end of the paragraph:

33–33   **Duration of duty.** When a reinsurance is placed in advance of insurance, and takes effect as a standing offer of reinsurance to be accepted by insurers agreeing to accept the underlying risks, the reinsured's duty of disclosure continues until the times at which the insuring underwriters have accepted the reinsurance—*Bonner v. Cox Dedicated Corporate Member Ltd.* [2005] Lloyd's Rep. I.R. 569.

Add to the end of the paragraph:

Materiality. The very nature of reinsurance means that facts not **33–34** encountered in primary insurance will be found to be material, such as whether the underlying insurance contract is a true contract of indemnity or is for payment of an agreed sum irrespective of the reinsured's actual loss— *Toomey v. Banco Vitalicio de Espana SA* [2004] Lloyd's Rep. I.R. 354; aff'd. on appeal [2005] Lloyd's Rep. I.R. 423, where the proportional nature of the reinsurance had the consequence that the liability of the reinsurers was proportional to the actual liability of the reassured. Conversely, a fact which would ordinarily be thought material, such as the occurrence of a substantial loss on the underlying insurance for which reinsurance was sought, has been held *obiter* to be immaterial to a fronting company which was concerned only with the solvency of the companies for which it fronted— *Bonner v. Cox Dedicated Corporate Member Ltd* [2005] Lloyd's Rep. I.R. 569—but with respect one wonders whether it ought nonetheless to be concerned about the materiality of the fact to the insurers for whom it fronts.

Add new paragraph as follows:

Full Reinsurance Clause. This is a standard composite clause dating back **33–52A** to at least 1943, containing three separate elements, (1) a "terms as original" provision, (2) a "follow the settlements" provision and (3) a retention stipulation with a blank space for a percentage figure to be inserted. In the present context we are concerned with the first element—"Being a reinsurance of and warranted same gross rate, terms and conditions as and to follow the settlements of the company [the reinsured]". There are at least two forms of this clause and it is frequently found in reinsurance contracts notwithstanding the uncomplimentary remarks made by the House of Lords concerning its drafting—*Forsikrings.Vesta v. Butcher* [1989] A.C. 852. Despite the use of the word "warranted", it is not a warranty by the reinsured that the underlying policy contains the same terms as those shown to the reinsurer, but rather gives effect to an agreement between the parties that, in consideration for the reinsured consenting that the terms of the original insurance are to be incorporated in the reinsurance contract in order to preclude the latter's liability from being affected by variations to the underlying contract, the reinsurer will follow the settlements of his reinsured—*Phoenix General Insurance v. ADAS* [1988] Q.B. 216, 278 *per* Kerr

LJ; *Forsikrings. Vesta v. Butcher* [1989] A.C. 852, 891, *per* Lord Templeman with whom three of their Lordships agreed; *Toomey v. Banco Vitalicio de Espana* [2004] Lloyd's Rep. I.R. 354 [78–90]; *Prifti v. Musini* [2004] Lloyd's Rep. I.R. 528 [17]. On appeal from the judgment in *Toomey*, the Court of Appeal refrained from expressing a view on the construction of the clause—[2005] Lloyd's Rep. I.R. 423. As will be seen, however, the incorporation element in the clause may well fail to achieve its objective, even though its inclusion in a reinsurance is indicative of an intention to make the reinsurance "back to back" with the underlying contract. An "as original" provision such as the Full Reinsurance Clause will not "work in reverse", that is to say, render ineffective an express term contained in the reinsurance but not contained in the primary insurance. So where a film finance facultative reinsurance contained a warranty that an identified individual should remain in the employment of the original assured company for a stated duration, but no such term was contained in the underlying policy, the inclusion of a full reinsurance clause in the reinsurance slip did not suffice to neutralise the warranty—*GE Reinsurance Corporation v. New Hampshire Insurance Co.* [2004] Lloyd's Rep. I.R. 404 [55].

Delete n.86 and replace as follows:

33–52   **The terms to be incorporated.** In *Forsikrings. Vesta v. Butcher* in the House of Lords, Lord Griffiths preferred to interpret the Full Reinsurance Clause in that case as a warranty by the reinsured that the underlying policy was or would be written in the same terms as those made available to the reinsurer at placement [1989] A.C. 852, 896. The other members of the House of Lords did not read it in this way—*Toomey v. Banco Vitalicio de Espana* [2004] Lloyd's Rep. I.R. 354 [84–85]. The point was left open on appeal—[2005] Lloyd's Rep. I.R. 423. However, both courts held that the statement of the nature of the original insurance in the reinsurance slip constituted a warranty on the part of the reinsured, and had been breached. This part of the judgment was affirmed on appeal—[2005] Lloyd's Rep. I.R. 423 [40–43]. For the Full Reinsurance Clause see paragraph 33–52A *post.*

Add to n.91:

33–54   **Intention as to incorporation.** A "follow the leader" clause in an underlying insurance is neither germane nor apposite to a facultative reinsurance—*American International Marine Agency v. Dandridge* [2005] 2 All E.R. (Comm) 496 [48].

Add to n. 92 after the reference to the Groupama Navigation case:
See also *American International Marine Agency v. Dandridge* [2005] 2 All
E.R. (Comm) 496 [20] and [40].

Add to n.97:

Germane to reinsurance. These authorities were relied upon in *Unum Life*   **33–56**
v. Israel Phoenix [2002] Lloyd's Rep. I.R. 374 at first instance for the proposition that, where a slip provides for "wording to be agreed by leading
reinsurer only", the leader cannot bind followers to an arbitration clause
which he agrees to be included in the wording. It is submitted that a clause
bestowing a mandate upon the leader to agree the final wording of the
reinsurance is entirely different from general words of incorporation, and
that this proposition is incorrect. An appeal to the Court of Appeal was
dismissed on other grounds, but Mance L.J. indicated more than a hint of
disagreement with it.

Add to n. 98:
Siboti v. BP France [2003] 2 Lloyd's Rep. 364 [40]; *Prifti v. Musini* [2004]
Lloyd's Rep. I.R. 528 [15].

Retitle this paragraph, delete existing text and replace as follows:

Alterations to the underlying policy. The purpose of a clause incorporating   **33–61**
the terms of an underlying insurance is often not merely to supplement the
terms expressly agreed for the reinsurance by a process of incorporation, but
to achieve an identical standard of liability on the two contracts. In *Lower
Rhine & Wurtemberg Insurance Association v. Sedgwick* [1899] 1 Q.B. 179, a
facultative marine reinsurance on the ship "Collynie" was expressed to be
"subject to the same terms, conditions and clauses as original policy or
policies whether reinsurance or otherwise, and to pay as may be paid
thereon". At that time, the reinsured was on risk under two primary hull
and machinery policies on the "Collynie" with a joint agreed valuation of
£5,600. The reinsurance contained the same valuation. The ship became an
ATL, and a claim was paid by the reinsurer without insisting on seeing the
underlying policies. Subsequently, his retrocessionaires insisted upon production of these, whereupon it emerged that the two underlying policies had
been replaced by one policy after the inception of the reinsurance and before
the loss, and which contained certain variations in the terms, the most
important being that the agreed value was lowered to £5,000. The reinsurer
brought proceedings for repayment of the policy monies as money paid
under a mistake of fact.
At first instance, Kennedy J. held that the reference to "original policy or

policies" was to those in being at the time of loss, so that the changed valuation did not make any difference to the reinsurance—[1898] 1 Q.B. 739. The Court of Appeal took a different view, holding that it referred to the underlying policies in force at the time of placement of the reinsurance. Their decision turned upon the perceived purpose of the "as original" clause, which was to make the reinsurance back-to-back with the primary insurance. On page 190 of the report, Collins L.J. referred to the closing words of the clause and said:

"This, as was pointed out, is the essence of the contract. Its purpose is to cover in whole or in part the risk actually undertaken on 'an original' policy. The standard of liability must be ascertained and identical in both cases. I do not mean that the whole sum underwritten must be covered by the reinsurance, neither need the whole risk. For instance, the original policy may cover any loss, partial or total; the reinsurance may be against total only or partial only; but the conditions under which one or the other can be recovered are to be identical, so that the payment on the reinsurance may be 'as paid' on the original".

In other words, the terms of the underlying insurance were the foundation of the facultative reinsurance so that the reinsurer was agreeing only to meet such liabilities as arose thereunder. The variations to the policies released the reinsurer from liability, because thereafter no claim could be brought on a policy with the same terms as the original, and his consent had not been given to the variations.

Insert new paragraphs as follows:

33–61A   The *Lower Rhine* case was followed in *Norwich Union Fire Insurance Society v. Colonial Mutual Fire Insurance Society* [1922] 2 K.B. 461. Here a vessel was insured against total loss only by the underlying marine policy. The insurers reinsured their risk under a facultative reinsurance in which the vessel was valued at the same sum as in the primary policy—£313,050 and containing an identical "subject to" clause as that construed in the earlier case. During the currency of both policies, the reinsured varied the underlying insurance by agreement with the assured, but without the consent of the reinsurer. In particular, the sum insured was reduced to £225,000. Thereafter, she became a total loss. McCardie J. held that the reinsurers were released from liability by the variations to the underlying policy, because their liability did not extend to claims arising under a policy on different terms from the original, and the underlying policy could only be altered by the reinsured with the consent of the reinsurer. He also referred to the doctrine of surety law that a variation in the terms of the creditor's contract with the debtor without the surety's consent discharges the surety without more, unless it is self-evident that it is neither material nor prejudicial to him, and held that, "a rule at least as rigorous should apply to matters of insurance".

In *HIH Casualty & General Insurance Ltd v. New Hampshire Insurance Co.* [2002] 2 Lloyd's Rep.161, the Court of Appeal was concerned with the interpretation of a clause in a quota share reinsurance policy which provided: **33–61B**

> "The Reinsured hereon agrees to consult and obtain Reinsurers' agreement to all amendments and alterations to the terms clauses and conditions of the Original Policy".

There was also a clause, making the reinsurance subject to all terms clauses and conditions as the original policy. The court held that the first clause was a warranty, and regarded it as reflecting the position at common law, for which the *Norwich Union* decision was cited [109]. It is clear that where the reinsurance contains a "subject" clause making the underlying insurance the basis of the reinsurance, any unauthorised variations to the latter will release the reinsurer from liability, unless they are immaterial, being self-evidently of no concern to the reinsurer, or as David Steel J. described it in the court below, not affecting the sense or substance of the underlying policy in a manner potentially prejudicial to the reinsurer—[2001] 1 Lloyd's Rep. 378, 385.

Add to text after n.13:

Similar interpretation. In *Goshawk Syndicate Management Ltd. v. XL Specialty Insurance Co.* [2004] 2 All E.R. (Comm) 512, coverage limits clauses in a facultative reinsurance were construed so as to result in a similar liability for insurers and reinsurers alike, because constant references to "all as original" demonstrated the common intention that both policies should be back-to-back.   **33–62**

Add new paragraph as follows:

"Loss arising from any one event". The foregoing authorities were analysed and discussed by the Court of Appeal in *Scott v. Copenhagen Reinsurance Co (UK) Ltd* [2003] 2 All E.R. (Comm) 190. The case concerned the application of aggregation provisions in a whole account excess of loss reinsurance to the loss of civilian aircraft, following the Iraqi invasion of Kuwait in August 1990. Iraqi forces took control of 15 Kuwait Airways aeroplanes based at the airport and one BA 747 aeroplane which happened to be there. The 15 Kuwaiti planes were quickly flown back to Iraq but the BA plane was left sitting at the airport until eventually it was destroyed in the course of Coalition bombing in February 1991. The reinsurance   **33–66A**

provided that "Loss" meant "loss, damage, liability or expense arising from any one event or as described in section J of the schedule". The schedule read: "Loss Description: each and every loss or series of losses arising from one event". The question for the Court was whether the loss of the BA 747 was to be aggregated with the loss of the 15 Kuwaiti aircraft. Essentially, this turned upon whether the loss of the BA 747 was one "arising from the same event" as the loss of the Kuwait Airways fleet.

Rix L.J. analysed the earlier decisions and held that the starting point was to identify a single unifying event, since that was the type of unifying factor selected as the link for purposes of aggregation. An event was to be distinguished from a state of affairs, following *Axa Reinsurance Plc v. Field* [1996] 1 W.L.R. 1026, 1035. It had to occur prior to the losses sought to be aggregated. There then had to be a significant causal relationship with the losses, as required by the words "arising from", so that a plurality of losses were to be regarded as a single aggregated loss, if sufficiently linked to a single unifying event by being causally related to it. The question then became: Was there one event which should be regarded as the cause of all these losses so as to make it appropriate to see them as one loss for purposes of aggregation? [68] Applying this causation test and the alternative "unities" test of whether the relevant losses shared a common time, place and cause, one came to the same answer. The loss of the BA plane was not caused by the capture of the airport. There was no intention on the part of the Iraqi Government to seize it. One could not say at that stage that it was lost to BA. It was necessary to "wait and see" how events unfolded after the invasion. The cause of its loss was either the war declared in January 1991, launched by the Coalition after lengthy diplomatic efforts to create a military coalition had succeeded, when it was for the first time placed in the line of fire, or its actual destruction in a bombing raid in the course of that war. Conversely, the Kuwaiti planes were lost at a different time by a different cause. There was unity of place only, and this was insufficient. At the end of the day the question of whether the losses arose from one event required the court to consider all the relevant facts and to conduct an exercise of judgment in order to come to an answer. [81–83]

Add new paragraph as follows:

33–69A In *Bonner v. Cox Dedicated Corporate Member Ltd* [2005] Lloyd's Rep. I.R. 569, it was held that no duty of care was owed by reinsureds to their reinsurers under excess of loss reinsurance contracts. The risk of the reinsured not exercising appropriate skill and care in underwriting particular risks was one which such reinsurers were bound to bear as part and parcel of that type of cover, as stated by Thomas J. in *Sphere Drake Insurance Co v. European International Underwriting* [2003] Lloyd's Rep. I.R. 525. It appears that the learned judge, Morison J, distinguished the *Phoenix* case, *supra*, on the basis that it concerned a proportional reinsurance leading to a presumption that risks would be written, as it were, for the common good. He also held, following *Sphere Drake Insurance Co v. European International Underwriting* [2003] Lloyd's Rep. I.R. 525, that there was no objection to an insurer making a profit at the expense of his reinsurers per se, but that the deliberate writing of loss-making business with the view of passing it on to reinsurers constituted the acceptance of business outside the scope of what was contemplated to be reinsured, rendering the reinsurance voidable for non-disclosure. Morison J also noted that a coverholder does not owe a duty of care to reinsurers in selecting risks, citing *Aneco v. Johnson & Higgins* [2002] 1 Lloyd's Rep. 157 and the *Sphere Drake* case cited *supra*. For comment see (2005) 17 Insurance Law Monthly Number 5, page 7.

Add new paragraph as follows:

In *Charman v. New Cap Reinsurance Corp.* [2004] 1 All E.R. (Comm) 114, **33–72A** a three-year reinsurance contract contained a premium review clause which provided that the reinsurer reserved the right to increase the annual premium at any anniversary date during the term if certain things happened, including if any "extraordinary claims developments" occurred. It claimed the right to do so after one year, but failed to justify the claim. No further notice of the claim was given, but a claim was subsequently made for additional premium in respect of the third year, the reinsurer claiming that the un-successful notice of the claim continued in force as a notice for later years and was ultimately re-energised by the occurrence of extraordinary claims development in the second year. It was held that the clause had to be expressly invoked to increase the premium at a particular anniversary date, and that it must give the reason for invoking it. It had never been stated that an increase was sought as of the end of the second year and it was impermissible to give an advance notice which would be relied upon in the event that extraordinary claims developments should be experienced. It was also held *obiter* that the nomination of a new premium was necessary to the valid invocation of the clause.

In sub-paragraph (a) delete the words "the claim so accepted" and replace **33–83** with "the claim so recognised".

Insert new paragraph as follows:

"Follow the settlements" clauses in back-to-back reinsurances. In *Assi-* **33–86A** *curazioni Generali v. CGU International Insurance Plc* [2004] 2 All E.R. (Comm) 114, the Court of Appeal considered the application of the first proviso in the definition of the reinsurer's liability given by Robert Goff L.J. in the *SCOR* case, cited at paragraph 33–83 above. *Generali* had settled a claim on a contractor's liability policy. 80% of their liability was reinsured by *CGU* under a reinsurance on back-to-back terms with the underlying insurance. The reinsurance was:

> "As original: ... subject to the same terms, clauses and conditions, special or otherwise, as the original policy or policies and is to pay as may be paid thereon and to follow without question the settlements of the Reassured except ex-gratia and/or without prejudice settlements"

Generali argued that the first proviso precluded reinsurers from raising coverage issues under the reinsurance, when that contract was on the same terms as the underlying insurance. This was because the coverage issues would echo those arising on the primary insurance, these had been settled, and such settlement was binding upon the reinsurers. The only exceptions would be if there was some defence special to the reinsurance which could not arise on the underlying insurance and in the present case, if the settlement was on ex-gratia or without prejudice terms. The Court of Appeal rejected this submission, following the judgment of Evans J. in *Hiscox v. Outhwaite (No 3)* [1991] 2 Lloyd's Rep. 524, and upheld the decision of Mr Kealey Q.C., Deputy-Judge, in the court below—[2003] 2 All E.R. (Comm) 425. The true position was that the reinsured did not need to prove that the claim was in fact covered by the underlying policy. It was sufficient to show that the claim which the reinsured had settled, as recognised by him, was arguably within the underlying policy. It followed that the reinsured then had to show that the basis upon which it was settled was one which fell within the reinsurance as a matter of law, or at least arguably did so. This and the requirement that the reinsured must have acted honestly and taken all reasonable and proper steps in settling the claim provided adequate protection for the reinsurer.

Generali also argued that the words "without question" excluded the second proviso in *SCOR*. This argument also failed, for reasons given by the learned deputy-judge. These were words of emphasis, and were insufficiently clear to deprive reinsurers of the valuable protection conferred upon them by the second proviso.

Add new paragraphs as follows:

33–90A   **Duty to inform reinsurers.** Sometimes claims control clauses appear under the title of claim co-operation clause. One such case is *Eagle Star Insurance Co Ltd v.Cresswell* [2004] Lloyd's Rep. I.R. 537. A reinsurance policy contained a printed Full Reinsurance Clause and a typed claims co-operation clause. The latter provided that :

> "The underwriters hereon shall control the negotiations and settlements of any claims under this policy. In this event the underwriters hereon will not be liable to pay any claim not controlled as set out above".

It was held that this clause constituted a condition precedent, not to all liability, but to liability in the event of there being negotiations or settlements. The first sentence allocated to reinsurers the right to control any negotiation or settlement which took place between Eagle Star and its assured. To this end, Eagle Star had to inform reinsurers when negotiations were about to begin, so that reinsurers could say what form these were to take and what offers were to be made. The reinsurers were therefore not liable to meet their share of a settlement which they had not controlled because they had not been informed that negotiations were afoot. The words "will not be liable to pay" in the last sentence of the clause related to the ultimate liability to pay the resulting claim and not just to the obligation in the full reinsurance clause to follow Eagle Star's settlements. Consequently, Eagle Star would not be able to recover even if they disclaimed reliance on the settlement itself and sought to prove their liability towards their assured independently of it. Although this was a severe construction of the clause, it was mitigated by the fact that the obligation imposed on Eagle Star was simple, by the possibility that reinsurers might waive their right to control a settlement negotiation, and by the implied term that the reinsurers were not to withhold approval of a settlement in bad faith, capriciously or arbitrarily, as held in *Gan Insurance Co. Ltd v. Tai Ping Insurance Co. Ltd (2 & 3)* [2001] Lloyd's Rep. I.R. 667. This decision demonstrates that the benefit of a following settlements clause is lost through the inclusion of claims control clauses, which effectively hand over the conclusion of the settlement to reinsurers.

Use of inappropriate claims control clause. In *Royal & Sun Alliance Insurance plc v. Dornoch Ltd* [2005] 1 All E.R. (Comm) 590, Royal & Sun Alliance reinsured its participation on the Directors & Officers Liability section of a Master Subscription Policy with several Lloyd's Syndicates. The reinsurance contained a Full Reinsurance Clause and a Claims Control Clause (CCL). The latter provided: **33–90B**

> "Notwithstanding anything herein contained to the contrary, it is a condition precedent to any liability under this policy that:
>
> (a) The Reinsured shall upon knowledge of any loss or losses which may give rise to claim under this policy, advise the Underwriters thereof by cable within 72 hours..."

By 12 December 2000, the reinsured knew that proceedings had begun by third parties alleging loss caused by misleading statements made by the original assureds. Copies of the court "complaints" were received on 30 December 2000. No advice of these matters was given to reinsurers until 19 January 2001 and the latter claimed to be under no liability to their reinsured. The Court of Appeal noted that the CCL was a standard clause which was obviously more apposite to a property damage policy. There was a mismatch between the original insurance, which was on a "claims made" basis and required notification of "claims", and the CCL which depended on knowledge of a loss on the part of the reinsured. Longmore L.J. commented:

> "But, however inapposite the clause may be, the court has to give it a sensible meaning in accordance with any helpful canons of construction which may be available" [10].

The first issue for the court was whether the reference to loss meant alleged loss or actual loss. If the clause was being used in its proper context of a property cover, it would be normal to construe it as alleged loss, although no doubt compliance would not be made a condition precedent. In the context of a liability policy, it made sense to read it as referring to an actual loss, as otherwise the strict time limit of 72 hours was unjustifiably draconian. It followed that even if the loss was assumed to be that of the third parties as opposed to that of the assured, the reinsured did not have knowledge of any actual loss suffered by the third party complainants in December 2000 or January 2001, and indeed they would not know it until a loss was proved or admitted, which was still in dispute. There was no breach of the CCL.

INSURANCE COMPANIES

1. BACKGROUND

Add at the end of the paragraph as follows:

E.C. directives on freedom of services. The three life insurance directives **34–7** were consolidated by Directive 2002/83/EC. Consequential changes to various statutes and statutory instruments were made by the Life Assurance Consolidation Directive (Consequential Amendments) Regulations 2004, (S.I. 2004 No. 3379).

2. REGULATION UNDER THE FINANCIAL SERVICES AND MARKETS ACT 2000

(e) *Transfers of Business and Winding Up*

Add at the end of the paragraph as follows:

As long as a scheme results in a transfer of business, there is no **34–30** requirement that it does anything else—*Re Norwich Union Linked Life Assurance Ltd* [2004] EWHC 2802 (Ch).

Add to n.97:

See also *Re Norwich Union Linked Life Assurance Ltd* [2004] EWHC 2802 (Ch) and *Re Allied Dunbar Assurance plc* [2005] 2 B.C.L.C. 220.

Add to n.1:

34–31   See also *Re Norwich Union Linked Life Assurance Ltd* [2004] EWHC 2802 (Ch).

(f) *Compensation and Continuity of Cover*

Add to n.65:

34–44   **Eligible Claimants.** The construction of the words "in respect of a liability subject to compulsory insurance", as they appeared in s. 6(5) of the Policyholders Protection Act 1975, were given a broad construction in *R. v. Financial Services Compensation Scheme, ex parte Geologistics Ltd* [2004] 1 W.L.R. 1719. They were descriptive of the type of liability covered by the policy and not intended to describe an actual established liability. In its context, the phrase "in respect of" was intended to mean or at least include "in connection with". As a result Financial Services Compensation Scheme was obliged to indemnify the assured against its own costs of defending a claim brought by an employee, as well as the damages awarded and the claimant employee's costs.

(g) *Dispute Resolution and Complaints*

Add at the end of the paragraph as follows:

34–58   **Determination of complaints.** It has been confirmed that the Ombudsman can make an award that differs from what a court, applying the law, would make, provided that he concluded that this was fair and reasonable in all the circumstances of the case and he had taken into account the matters identified in rule 3.8.1(2)—*R. v. Financial Ombudsman Services Ltd, ex parte IFG Financial Services Ltd* [2005] EWHC 1153 (Admin).

CHAPTER 35

THE COURSE OF BUSINESS AT LLOYD'S

1. REGULATION OF THE LLOYD'S MARKET

Add at the end of the paragraph as follows:

The role of the Society and the Financial Services Authority. Lloyd's is not   **35–2**
a public body and hence decisions made by it are not amenable to challenge
by way of judicial review—*R. v. Lloyd's of London, ex parte West* [2004]
Lloyd's Rep. I.R. 755. In so holding, the Court of Appeal followed a
number of earlier decisions to the same effect, decided before the passing of
the Human Rights Act 1988 (*R. v. Lloyd's of London, ex parte Briggs* [1993]
1 Lloyd's Rep. 176, *R. v. Corporation of Lloyd's, ex parte Lorimer*, 1992,
unreported and *R. v. Council of Society of Lloyd's, ex parte Johnson*, 1996,
unreported) and confirmed that, Lloyd's not being a body exercising public
functions within the meaning of section 6 of that Act, that was still the
position. The judgment of Brooke L.J. contains a most lucid description of
the structure of Lloyd's and its relationship with the Financial Services
Authority. This decision was followed in a case where a claim for mis-
feasance in public office was struck out—*Society of Lloyd's v. Henderson*
[2005] EWHC 850 (Comm).

Add at the end of the paragraph as follows:

Responsibilities of managing agents. Failure to comply with the formal   **35–6**
requirements under the Lloyd's bye laws for the execution of an agreement

does not render the agreement in any way void or illegal—*P & B Ltd v. Woolley* [2002] Lloyd's Rep. I.R. 344.

2. PLACING INSURANCE AT LLOYD'S

Add to n.53:

35–13   **Payment of the premium.** That the usage is inapplicable to non-marine insurance was confirmed in *Goshawk Dedicated Ltd v. Tyser & Co. Ltd* [2005] Lloyd's Rep. I.R. 379.

3. PAYMENT OF LOSSES UNDER LLOYD'S POLICIES

Add at the end of the paragraph as follows:

35–35   In *Goshawk Dedicated Ltd v. Tyser & Co. Ltd* [2005] Lloyd's Rep. I.R. 379, Lloyd's syndicates claimed the right to inspect and copy various placing documents, claims documents and premium accounting documents in the possession of the Lloyd's brokers. The latter argued that the syndicates were not entitled to see these unless their clients, the assureds, consented. The documents related first to policies placed before new terms of business agreements ("T.O.B.A.") (required by the Lloyd's Broker Byelaw 17/2000) were agreed on December 20, 2001 and secondly to policies placed after that date. The claims in respect of all the documents for policies written prior to that date were rejected, Christopher Clarke J. finding no implied agreement or custom that supported them and, in any event, holding that any such would be unreasonable as contrary to the authorities discussed in the preceding paragraphs. The position with regard to policies placed after December 20, 2001 was more complicated because of conflicting provisions in the T.O.B.A. Clause 8 provided that the broker agreed to allow the managing agent on reasonable notice to inspect and take copies of (1) accounting records and (2) various documents relating to the proposal, the placing and any claims. However, clause 2.2 provided that "Nothing in this agreement overrides the broker's duty to place the interests of its client before all other considerations." The learned judge held that, so far as post-2001 placing and claims documents were concerned, clause 2.2 "trumped" clause 8; brokers were not obliged to hand over documents without their client's consent. However, the syndicate was entitled to see post-2001 accounting documents because the brokers could not have any genuine reason to fear that this could be against the interests of their clients.

CHAPTER 36

THE ROLE OF AGENTS IN INSURANCE BUSINESS

2. THE ASSURED'S AGENT

Add to n.74:

Introductory. See also *European International Reinsurance Co. Ltd v.* **36–22**
Curzon Insurance Ltd [2003] Lloyd's Rep. I.R. 793.

Add to n.80:

Duty of agent to client. This will now clearly include the Insurance Con- **36–23**
duct of Business Rules promulgated by the Financial Services Authority; see
paras. 36–76 *et seq., post.*

Add to n.83:

Liability for failure to effect insurance. As to the possibility of the agent **36–25**
bringing proceedings for a contribution claim under the Civil Liability
(Contribution) Act 1978 against a party who might also be liable to the
assured, see *Hurstwood Developments Ltd v. Motor & General & Andersley &*
Co. Ins. Services Ltd [2002] Lloyd's Rep. I.R. 185.

Add at end of paragraph as follows:

36–29   **Expedition.** Similarly, an agent may be liable for failing to make proper notification to the insurers—*Alexander Forbes Europe Ltd v. SBJ Ltd* [2003] Lloyd's Rep. I.R. 432.

Add to n.31:

36–39   Compare *Alexander Forbes Europe Ltd v. SBJ Ltd* [2003] Lloyd's Rep. I.R. 432 (no reduction).

4. STATUTORY AND PROFESSIONAL REGULATION

Add at the end of the paragraph as follows:

36–72   The self-regulatory scheme was duly replaced by a statutory scheme with effect from January 2005. See new paragraph 36–76, *post*.

Add new paragraphs as follows:

36–76   **Statutory regulation of general insurance intermediaries.** The G.I.S.C. scheme described in the previous paragraph ceased to operate when the statutory scheme, introduced pursuant to the Insurance Mediation Directive (2002/92/EC), was introduced by the Insurance Mediation Directive (Miscellaneous Amendments) Regulations 2003 (S.I. 2003 No. 1473) and the Financial Services and Markets Act 2000 (Regulated Activities) (Amendment) (No. 2) Order 2003 (S.I. 2003 No. 1476). The latter amended the Financial Services and Markets Act 2000 (Regulated Activities) Order 2001 (S.I. 2001 No. 2635) to that, subject to the exceptions mentioned below, activities regulated by section 22 of the 2000 Act (see paragraph 34–16, *ante*) include buying or selling rights under contracts of insurance as agent, making arrangements for other persons to buy contracts of insurance and assisting in the administration and performance of a contract of insurance (other than expert appraisal, loss adjusting or claims management) in the course of a profession or business. So, the Financial Services Authority (F.S.A) now regulates the activities of all insurance intermediaries (both on the general market and at Lloyd's), except in respect of travel insurance sold as part of a holiday package and the insurance of large risks (as to these, see paragraph 34–7, *ante*, footnote 24) and reinsurance. The detail is to be found in the Principles for Business and the Insurance Conduct of Business Rules (I.C.O.B.) produced by the F.S.A. and, so far as concerns the competence of individuals, the Fit and Proper Test for Approved Persons Sourcebook. I.C.O.B. draws a distinction between retail customers and commercial customers. Retail customers are natural persons acting for purposes outside their trade, business or profession. Commercial customers are any other persons, although small businesses do receive some extra protection as regards product disclosure and advice. A further consequence of this regulation is that complaints against intermediaries are now within the jurisdiction of the Financial Ombudsman Service (see paragraphs 34–53 *et seq, ante*). They key requirements of I.C.O.B., rules 4 and 5, are outlined in the following paragraphs.

General. Intermediaries are required to take reasonable steps to ensure **36–77** that, if they make any personal recommendation to customers to buy insurance, the recommendation is suitable for their customers' demands and needs at this time. In order to do this, they are required to seek such information about customers' circumstances and objectives, as might reasonably be expected to be relevant, in enabling them to identify customers' requirements.

Disclosure of information. Intermediaries are required to disclose a num- **36–78** ber of matters, including their statutory status, the kind of advice they are willing to offer, whether they will seek terms from more than one insurer and their complaints procedure (including mention of the Financial Ombudsman Service). This must be disclosed in a "durable medium" before conclusion of an insurance contract, unless customers require immediate cover or the contract is made by telephone, in which case oral disclosure suffices. Intermediaries are also required to explain the duty to disclose material information both before the contract commences and throughout its duration, and the consequences of a failure to disclose. Further retail customers must also be supplied with, *inter alia*, a summary of any policy proposed and a statement of the premium. Their attention must also be drawn orally to the summary and the section on "significant and unusual exclusions or limitations." On conclusion of the contract, they must be supplied in a durable medium with a policy document, information about the claims handling process and, where relevant, cancellation rights. Renewal notices must also be sent, where relevant.

Commission. Intermediaries are required to disclose to commercial cus- **36–79** tomers, but not to retail customers, and only if requested, the commission they receive in cash terms or, to the extent that it cannot be indicated in cash, the basis for the calculation of the commission.